Cries from the Heart

JOHANN CHRISTOPH ARNOLD

Cries from the Heart

Stories of
Struggle
and
Hope

Plough Publishing House

Published by Plough Publishing House
Walden, New York
Robertsbridge, England
Elsmore, Australia
www.plough.com

© 1999, 2001 by Plough Publishing House
All Rights Reserved.

First Edition 1999
Second Edition 2001
20 19 18 17 16 15   4 5 6 7 8 9 10 11

ISBN 10: 0-87486-980-3
ISBN 13: 978-0-87486-980-4

Cover photograph © Paul Clancy

A catalog record for this book is available from the British Library.
Library of Congress Cataloging-in-Publication Data

Arnold, Johann Christoph, 1940–
    Cries from the heart : stories of struggle and hope / Johann
Christoph Arnold ; foreword by Robert Coles.
    p. cm.
  ISBN: 0-87486-980-3
    1. Christian life–Bruderhof Communities authors 2.
Prayer–Bruderhof Communities I. Title.
  BV4501.2 .A734 1999
  248.8'6–dc21
                                                            99-14692
                                                                CIP

Printed in the USA

Let each of us cry out to God as if we were hanging by a hair, and a tempest were raging to the very heart of heaven, and we had almost no more time left to cry out. For in truth, we are always in danger in the world, and there is no counsel and no refuge, save to lift up our eyes and hearts, and cry out to God.

Martin Buber

contents

to the reader — xi

foreword by Robert Coles — xiii

1. searching — *God finds an atheist* — 1

2. finding — *is someone really there?* — 9

3. believing — *even when children die?* — 15

4. universality — *call it what you will* — 23

5. god's messengers — *angels at work* — 33

6. emotional suffering — *when you can't pray* — 41

7. illness — *where the doctor leaves off* — 51

8. despair — *talking to a wall* — 65

9. attitude — *thank God I'm not like that!* — 79

10. reverence — *meet your maker* — 91

11. letting go — my *will be done* — 101

12. remorse — *when you've messed up* — 111

13. protection — *alive to tell it* — 123

14. selflessness — *someone needs you* — 131

15. service — *words are not enough* — 137

16. contemplation — *be quiet and listen* — 147

17. worship — *giving thanks in a death camp* — 159

18. unity — *divided we fall* — 165

19. marriage — *unlocking horns* — 171

20. unanswered prayer — *isn't "no" an answer?* — 181

21. miracles — *what do you expect?* — 189

22. prayer in daily life — *keeping the faith* — 203

23. faithfulness — *one thing never changes* — 213

to the reader

Johann Christoph Arnold

Since time began, people have sought for meaning and purpose in their lives, and even today, despite the rampant materialism of our culture, this is so. Some of us look to science and technology, others to religion and the supernatural; some of us look upward to a higher power, others within.

Whatever our beliefs, all of us sense that somewhere there must be answers to the age-old questions of suffering and death, life and love. Sometimes we may stumble on these answers; at other times they are yielded with learning, with experience, with the passing of years. Sometimes they come only with intense struggle – with cries from the heart.

In my work as counselor and pastor over forty years, I have met hundreds of people whose lives were enriched by their search for life's deepest answers. Though the particulars of their stories may not be important, the pattern they reveal is. In its own way, each shows that courage is rarely won without despair, that joy is often yoked with pain, and that faith is seldom reached without struggle and doubt.

There is hardly a story in this book that does not mention prayer, and none that does not in some way refer to faith in God. But even if you don't count yourself religious, don't be too quick to put it down. No matter your background, I am confident that the wisdom of the men and women in this book will give you something to take away—at very least, new eyes to see the path your life is taking.

Rifton, New York

foreword

Robert Coles

In the book you are about to read, you will find a stirring collection of personal accounts compiled by a most thoughtful and compassionate writer. Certainly, the men and women who divulge them are ordinary people. Yet that is not a weakness, but a strength. Even where you may not identify with their particulars, you will become, through hearing what they have to say, a participant in their ongoing search for wisdom, purpose, direction. As people whose stories prompt recognition of your own bouts with aspiration and despair, they invite your understanding as kindred souls, your embrace as fellow travelers.

Thankfully, the anecdotes in *Cries from the Heart* are rendered without contrivance: Arnold simply immerses the reader in them. Then, modestly and naturally, he invests them with larger meaning by using them to illustrate his theme: the universal human urge to find worthy answers to the great riddle of existence.

No wonder, then, that this book is more than the sum of its stories, more than a didactic assemblage of experiences. An unusually telling witness to the power of answered (or unanswered) yearning, it will summon you to new hope and call you to a reawakening of the mind and heart.

Cambridge, Mass.

1.

s e a r c h i n g

I was only seventeen when I first met Sibyl. A sophis-
ticated, articulate New Yorker, she was unforgettable in her
bright red dress and in her determination to prove there was
no goodness in the world.

My story is a typical atheist's story. We come into the
world with a preconceived idea. It's as if we had a pre-birth
memory of better days. By the time I was fourteen years
old, I knew the place was a mess. I was talking to God:
"Look, I think I'll live through parental arguing even if I
am an only child who has to carry it alone on her shoulders.
But those innocent children lying, fly-covered, in gutters in
India—I could do a better job!"

I was born in 1934, five years after the crash of 1929, and
maybe people were just gloomy in those days. Anyway,
on my fourth birthday I was presented with the ritual cake
and told I would get my wish should all the candles go out
in one blow. I took this as a guaranteed pipeline to that
Person I seemed to have known in pre-natal days. I instinc-
tively knew you didn't have to pepper him with details so,
after one successful blow, I told him to "make it all better,"
period.

Of course nothing got better. If anything, it got worse.
At four-and-a-half I attended my first Sunday-school class.
Upon being told where we were going, I thought, "At last,

a chance to meet God face to face." A miserable Sibyl met her parents on return. "How did you like Sunday school, dear?" "Awful. We cut out white sheep and pasted them on green paper." Organized, institutional religion never recouped itself in my eyes.

From that point on life was just something to be endured. There was nothing I or anyone else could do about it. As the only child of educated parents, I lived in commandeered luxury. It took only one "horror" a year to keep me shuddering at the prospect of coming to terms with the immense philosophical questions that plagued me. During my grade-school years, the blood-covered face of a drunk who was staggering upright. ("It's all right, dear, he just bumped his head. He's fine.") Hearing about newborn puppies on whom some boys were doing bee-bee gun practice. Running into a flasher after wandering away from my mother in the supermarket. And ultimately, at eleven, seeing "by mistake" the beginning frames of a newsreel showing American forces entering German concentration camps after World War II. My mother and I groaned and covered our eyes, but I had already seen too much.

At fourteen, I had come to the end of my tether, inwardly. My perpetual demand to God for an utterly perfect world had gone unanswered. There was an overabundance of badness and, worst of all, I was beginning to see that the goodness was about ninety-five percent phony. Since the age of ten I had been methodically reading all the books in our house. I started out with *The Diary of a London Prostitute*. Other books I recall were Mailer's *The Naked and the Dead*, Sloan Wilson's *The Man in the Grey Flannel Suit*, and *Black Boy,* by Richard Wright. If my parents were reading provocative stuff like this, they weren't the parents I thought they were. In fact, these books were in every house in town. But they made no dent in anyone's life. Or did they?

I decided to give God one last chance. In California, a three-year-old was trapped in a narrow drainpipe she had fallen into. The entire nation prayed for her safe release, as men and machines tried to extract her without harming her in the process. It was time for a showdown. This is it, God, your last chance. Get her out alive, or we're finished. Look, if it were left to me, I'd save her without even being worshiped. The girl died in the pipe.

That did it. The last shreds of my regard for God were gone. Now I knew we were only animated blobs of protoplasm.

Then there was the idiocy of human morality, which appeared to be deeply rooted in "what the neighbors would think." And what the neighbors thought depended on where you lived. Morals, ethics, right and wrong – they were all purely cultural phenomena. Everyone was playing the game. I opted for nihilism and sensuality, and lived accordingly. Out with good and evil, out with morality of any kind, out with accepted cultural customs. A line from a movie summed it up: "Live fast, die young, and have a good-looking corpse." So I proceeded to live my beliefs, preaching them to any idiot who "believed." I smoked hard, drank hard, and lived hard. But I could not suppress a wrenching, clawing feeling that there might be a meaning to life, after all. In retrospect I see that I was so hungry, so aching for God, that I was trying to taunt him out of the clouds.

I spent my last two years of high school at Emma Willard, a private school for girls, where I had two close friends. One was a suburban Republican WASP, so intelligent she later went mad. The other was a Baltimore-born black of NAACP descent. Endlessly we discussed philosophy, read books, worked on the God question, reaffirmed our atheism, and read C.S. Lewis so that, just in case we should meet him, we'd be ready to "cut him down."

Chapel attendance was required at Emma Willard. I refused to bow my head during prayers as a matter of conscience, but was caught and admonished. My punishment? Banishment to the back row, where I sat defiantly reading Freud.

Radcliffe College seemed as phony as church, and I soon dropped out and got married. Born in Madrid to a famous novelist, my husband, Ramón, was orphaned as a small boy along with his baby sister when Fascists executed their mother during the Spanish Civil War. When the New York PEN Club heard they needed rescuing, a well-to-do member offered to take the children in. Ramón's childhood was even more luxurious than mine, but it meant just as little to him as mine to me.

Both bent on escaping the stultifying atmosphere of dull riches, we felt the kindred soul in each other when we met in 1951 or 52. In 1954 we dropped out of our colleges to marry. Each of us was nineteen.

We very soon ran out of money. For two ex-rich kids it was "an experience." Wedding presents were pawned. It was sad, but we had to admit that money must be acquired at times.

The first crack in my hardened heart occurred after the birth of my daughter, Xaverie. She was so innocent – just like the hundred other babies in the maternity ward of the big New York City hospital she was born in. I wept inwardly, thinking that in fifty years half of them will be dying in the gutter, the other half rich and miserable. Why are such pure beings put here on this terrible earth?

While nursing her at night, I steeped myself in Dostoyevsky. Truths were coming at me, but I couldn't have defined them then. There wasn't time for philosophical musings anyway. By the time that baby girl, Xaverie, turned one, there was no father in the house. Ramón was coming and going, and a powerful, new force – the survival instinct called mother love – was taking hold of me. Get a job, get a babysitter, pay the rent, find a new husband. The babysitter plus rent left $10 a week for food and transportation. Not that I let anyone feel sorry for "the poor young mother." I was a rotten wife who was reaping what she had sown. I knew Ramón and I bore equal blame, and if I were him, I would have left me too.

My life descended steadily into the swineherd's berth. Ramón and I were going through what I considered our final separation. I was currently "in love" with another man, and I was carrying his child, which he wanted me to abort. I kept hoping he would change his mind at the last minute, but that never happened. So I, tough atheist that I was, went through with the most devastating ordeal of my life. Though still dedicated to the proposition that there was no such thing as "right and wrong" (no one had been able to persuade me otherwise), I was burdened with guilt beyond description.

There soon came a time when I was sure that short of my own death (Xaverie was all that stood between suicide and me), I had reached as close to the bottom as a person could get. It was on a hot August night in 1957, in surroundings I will not describe, that I groaned to a Being I did not believe in: "Okay, if there's really another way, show me."

Ramón startled me when he walked into my Manhattan office. A year earlier, he had left me to join the Beat Generation – Jack Kerouac, Allen Ginsberg, et al. – in San Francisco, and we'd not seen each other since. I was settled in Queens, across the street from my parents, and was working as an editor for a glossy magazine. I should have known Ramón could glide past the receptionist without question. No one in the office knew we were estranged, no one knew that this was but the most recent in a steady series of separations. He evoked no twinge of love in me.

Ramón launched into his story, the long and short of which was that he had discovered a religious commune upstate, that he felt drawn to it, and that he wanted me to visit it with him.

I couldn't think of a worse idea. As a professional atheist, I abhorred the religious. They were people whose faces froze in disapproving grimaces, who worried about their reputation for neatness and niceness, who never said, "C'mon in and have a cup of coffee and a cigarette." The religious were stiff and contrived and self-conscious. They seemed to be waiting for you to notice how good they were. Aside from that, there was Ramón. I wanted nothing more to do with him. He persisted. Eventually I agreed.

I picked my traveling clothes carefully. My fire-engine red, knit tube dress – that ought to ensure immediate rejection. All the way up from the City, my venom brewed. Then we were suddenly there, rounding the last curve and stopping under huge trees bearing swings for children. Xaverie made a beeline for them. It was October, and the colors were breathtaking, like a premonition of something good where I had hoped for something bad. I took twenty steps into the heart of the community and my resolve crumbled. "What if there *is* a God, after all?"

I tried not to show it, hoped it would pass. A woman came to meet me – peaceful, with loving eyes, a soft, makeup-less face. She didn't even notice that I was evil incarnate in a red dress. Nothing was working. She greeted me as if we were long-parted friends, seemed ready to be my sister for life. All this in a nanosecond.

But I wasn't ready to leap into the burning bush, not me. There was always hope that, in a minute, everything would reveal itself to be utterly phony.

The heavens and hells I lived through in the next forty-eight hours were as several entire lifetimes. Half my being was moved to tears; the other half scorned my reaction and reminded me that I was probably surrounded by mindless adults—a sort of spiritual schizophrenia.

On Sunday morning I looked forward to surcease in the battle. Surely the worship service would cure me of the strange leanings toward "goodness" I was feeling. It would be like every other nonsensical religious powwow I'd been to. Empty.

Entering the meeting room, however—the same room in which I'd already eaten three meals—I was struck dumb. Tables were shoved back, the kitchen chairs arranged in a circle. People were wearing their normal faded jeans and skirts, and there wasn't a shred of religious stuff to be seen. Someone was speaking, but it was just some guy in a farmer outfit. But then: horrors! He wasn't speaking. He was reading Dostoyevsky! It couldn't be! God, don't do this to me, I said to myself; don't hit me in the literary solar plexus. It was *The Brothers Karamazov*, and Ivan the intellectual was telling Alyosha the believer that he, Ivan, refuses to believe in a God who would countenance the torment of even one innocent child. Worlds, galaxies collided; it was my spiritual denouement. Quietly I accepted and then embraced a new question: Is it God who torments the innocent, or is it Sibyl?

Where Sibyl ended up is unimportant; how she got there is. As she says now, her doubting and yearning, her searching and rebelling—even if she was unaware of it at the time—were unspoken prayers. And God finally answered.

2.

finding

More than ever before, people are alone. If not physically separated from others, they are certainly more isolated emotionally. This is one of the great curses of our time: people are lonely and disconnected, depression is rampant, more marriages than ever are dysfunctional, and a pervasive sense of aimlessness marks many lives. Why *are* we here on earth? I believe that the answer to this question can only be discovered when we begin to find each other – and, more than that, to find God.

Each of us needs to find God, since our "vertical" relationship with him is always a strong determinant of our "horizontal" human relationships. But what does it mean to find God? Sibyl, whose story is in the previous chapter, says that for her it was "like finding a pearl."

> I was utterly consumed by my joy, as one in love. And once I found God, I saw the people around me – even though they were just normal human beings like myself – in a new light, and sharing life with them was like participating in an ongoing adventure. I continued to go through struggles, but they were punctuated by laughter, of all things. Before I found God I was sure that it would mean living a life of gloomy introspection, but what I found was prayer, forgiveness, love.

Sometimes it seems that the word "prayer" carries too much religious baggage with it; it is worn out from too much handling by too many people. It has become a duty that people feel they must fulfill, and therefore even a burden to rebel against. Personally, I do not see prayer as a duty, but an opportunity to come before God and tell him my worries, my needs, my happiness, or my gratitude. In this sense, prayer is simply conversing with God—something anyone can do.

Prayer may be a rite that involves a written verse, a prayer book, a certain place and time of day, or even a specific position of the body. Or it may have no form at all, but simply be a posture of the heart.

For most of us, silence and solitude are the most natural starting points for finding God and communicating with him, since both entail laying aside external distractions and emptying our minds and hearts of trivial concerns. It is as if God has come into the room to talk with us, and we must first look up from whatever we are doing to acknowledge him before the conversation can begin. For others of us, the act of becoming silent before God is not only a preparation for prayer, it *is* prayer. Such conversation is like the unspoken dialogue between a couple, or any other two people who know each other so well that they can communicate without words.

Naturally a true conversation has both sound and silence, give and take, talking and listening. Yet it is clear that God does not desire self-centered prattling: he knows what we need even before we ask. And if we do not become inwardly quiet, how will we ever be able to hear anything but our own voice? Nor does he require long, wordy petitions. If our hearts are truly turned to him, a glance upward or a heartfelt sigh, a moment of silence or a joyous song, a tearful plea or anguished weeping will do just as well. Each of these can be just as much a prayer as any number of carefully chosen words. Indeed, they may be more.

There are many ways to pray. One woman I know told me that she envisioned herself in prayer "like a baby bird in a nest with my head stretched way up and my oversized mouth open and hungry to receive whatever my father would drop into it. Not questioning, not doubting, not worrying, just receiving and totally appreciative."

Vemkatechwaram Thyaharaj, a friend from India, says:

I pray silently. All the same, though brought up as a Hindu Brahmin, I do not pray to an abstract being, but to the biblical Creator of the universe and of man—to God the Father. He is not distant from his creation, for Christ brought him down, close to man. It is to him I pray…

Very often I resort to lonely places for prayer. In such times I experience the divine, unseen touch that imparts power and life to my body and soul. True, it is always an effort to get out of bed early, before dawn. But this has been my practice, to sit during the early morning in the presence of God when I meditate and pray. During such times my heart is filled with peace and unexplainable joy.

Vemkatechwaram touches on an important aspect of genuine prayer: insofar as it is a conversation, it is not a vague state of being, but something that moves or takes place between two or more people, even if without words.

According to the early church father Tertullian, praying is also more than directing emotions or feelings toward God. It means experiencing his reality as a power.

Prayer has power to transform the weak, to restore the sick, to free the demon-possessed, to open prison doors, and to untie the bonds that bind the innocent. Furthermore, it washes away faults and repels temptations. It extinguishes persecutions. It consoles the low in spirit, and cheers those in good spirits. It escorts travelers, calms waves, and makes robbers stand aghast. It feeds the poor and governs the rich. It raises those who have fallen, stops others from falling, and strengthens those who are standing.

Tertullian also refers to prayer as the "fortress of faith" and the "shield and weapon against the foe." And Paul, in his Letter to the Ephesians, admonishes his fellow Christians to put on the "whole armor of God" and thereby enlist the aid of the Creator himself in times of trial.

Valid as these metaphors may be, it is good to remember that even if God's power can protect, shield, and comfort us, it is also a power before which we must sometimes quake. Especially after we have failed or done wrong, the act of coming to God in prayer and bringing our weaknesses to him means placing ourselves under his clear light, and seeing the wretchedness of our true state.

> Our God is a consuming fire, and my filth crackles as he seizes hold of me; he is all light and my darkness shrivels under his blaze. It is this naked blaze of God that makes prayer so terrible. For most of the time, we can persuade ourselves we are good enough, as good as the next man, perhaps even better, who knows? Then we come to prayer—real prayer, unprotected prayer—and there is nothing left in us, no ground on which to stand.
>
> *Sr. Wendy Beckett*

Given Sister Wendy's recognition of the contrast between the Almighty and a puny human being, one might fairly ask, "Does God really answer me, or does my praying just get me used to the discomfort of my situation?" Indeed, there are skeptics who feel that prayer is simply a forum for working through our feelings, and those who say, "All I want is God's will, and he can give that without my prayers."

I have no simple answers to these riddles, but that doesn't mean there are no answers. As I see it, it is a matter of relationship. If I claim God as my father, I need to be able to talk to him when I am in trouble. And before that, I need to be actively involved in my relationship with him — at least enough to know where I can find him.

Having given us free will, God does not force himself on any of us. He needs us to ask him to work in our lives before he intervenes. We must want his presence, be desperate for the inner food he can provide. Like the figures found on the walls of Roman catacombs, we must lift our eyes and arms to God, not merely waiting for him, but reaching upward to find him and to receive whatever he will give us.

In this sense praying is much more than talking with God. Prayer gives us the opportunity to discern God's will by coming into direct contact with him. It enables us to ask God for whatever we need, including judgment, mercy, and the grace to change our lives. It is even, as Henri Nouwen has written, "a revolutionary matter, because once you begin, you put your entire life in the balance."

3.

believing

Much has changed in the last hundred or so years since Robert Browning penned his famous lines, "God's in his Heaven / All's right with the world." Not many of us have such a cheerful view of things on our planet today. Indeed, because of the happenings of the last century, countless people have turned from faith, doubting the very existence of both God and heaven.

Certainly, we cannot show or see the God we worship. He is God for us just because we can know him but cannot see him. In his works, in all the movements of the universe, we perceive his power always, whether in thunder, lightning, an approaching storm, or in the clear sky.

And you believe that this God knows nothing of the doings and dealings of men? You believe that from his throne in heaven he cannot visit all men or know individual men? Man, in this you are mistaken and deceived. How can God be far away! The whole heaven and the whole earth and all things beyond the confines of the world are filled with God. Everywhere he is very close to us, yes, much more than that, he is in us. Look at the sun again! Fixed in the sky, its light is still poured out over all the earth. It is equally present everywhere and penetrates everything. Its splendor is nowhere dimmed. How much more is God present, he who is the creator of all things and sees all things, from whom nothing can remain hidden!

Minucius Felix, 3rd century

God. The very word implies belief, for if we cannot see, we must believe. Our senses, which so marvelously apprise us of our surroundings, are utterly useless when dealing with the unseen. But how is it with joy? With sorrow? Just because they cannot be seen, heard, or touched, is their existence denied? No, for our experience of them is so strong, and their effects so tangible, that we have no difficulty accepting them as reality.

So it is with God, he whom we know and love but do not fully understand. Who is he? Our very notions of him seem full of contradictions. Despite his invisible nature, he is eminently visible. He is so great, yet so small; creator as well as destroyer; immeasurably loving, yet stern. God sees all and moves all, yet is himself unseen and unchangeable. Desmond Tutu quotes a Bantu verse that puts this well:

In the beginning was God,
Today is God,
Tomorrow will be God.
Who can make an image of God?
He has no body.
He is the word that comes out of your mouth.
That word! It is no more,
It is past, and still it lives!
So is God.

And which one of us has not, in distress or anger if not in joy, lifted a voice to God? Perhaps it has been only in a vain hope that if he is there, he might – just possibly – pay attention to our pleading. But that is the beginning.

Prayer, as I noted in the previous chapter, is often no more than a sigh, a yearning of the heart, an expression of one's need for help. As such, it is also an acknowledgment, even if subconscious, of a being greater than ourselves.

Polls tell us that the majority of Americans pray daily, and almost all of these have experienced satisfactory answers to prayer. What does this mean? Can we conclude that this is a nation of God-fearing souls who love their neighbors as themselves? Hardly. But it tells us that, at least in the privacy of the home, many do turn to God. And apparently they have found a deep inner dimension to their own selves, a dimension that is hidden in the soul of every person, latent, waiting to be awakened.

Ron, an acquaintance whose sister was murdered, was justifiably angry: at God, at society, and at his sister's killer. But underneath it all, there was more:

> I probably prayed on and off my whole life, even though I didn't really know it. I guess I was just talking with God... I was at the bottom. I was ready to kill myself; I really was. And I got down on my knees and asked God to come into my life. He answered my prayer: he just didn't say anything. It was the way things changed, I knew he had answered me...I wasn't angry anymore.

Poet Jane Kenyon, who recently died of leukemia, wrote that she and her husband got into the habit of going to church because that is what their neighbors expected of them. Kenyon soon realized how spiritually empty she was. "Before I knew what had happened to me, I'd become a believer, not in the frightening God of my childhood, but in a God who, if you ask, forgives you no matter how far down in the well you are. If I didn't believe that, I couldn't live."

I like to think of belief as a child slipping her small hand into the welcoming hand of her father or mother. Many emotions and experiences are expressed in that simple act, but perhaps the most basic is "connectedness." Hand in hand, we establish a bond of trust and love. There are times when something within us makes it difficult to reach out with our hand, and it becomes an effort to accept the waiting hand. But when we do, what a relief comes over us! Now we are able to pour out our hearts, and God can work in us. Now we are ready to hear his answer.

How is it possible to find such inner certainty? Because God works in each individual in a unique way, each one will respond differently to his prompting and prodding. For most of us, faith will not come easily. More often given than earned, it may be elusive, too. One day it may seem to drop into our laps; the next, we may have to struggle to hold on to it. When the going is rough, this may seem discouraging. Yet as novelist Flannery O'Connor once suggested in a letter she wrote to a young friend, there is no such thing as belief without doubt or struggle.

> I think the experience of losing your faith, or of having lost it, is an experience that in the long run belongs to faith; or at least it can belong to faith if faith is still valuable to you, and it must be or you would not have written me about this.
>
> I don't know how the kind of faith required of a Christian living today can be at all if it is not grounded on this experience that you are having right now of unbelief. Peter said, "Lord, I believe. Help my unbelief." It is the most natural and most human and most agonizing prayer in the gospels, and I think it is the foundation prayer of faith.

A friend once wrote to the poet Gerard Manley Hopkins and asked him to tell him how he could believe. He must have expected a long philosophical answer. Hopkins wrote back, "Give alms." Perhaps he was trying to say that God is to be experienced in Charity (in the sense of love for the divine image in human beings). Don't get so entangled with intellectual difficulties that you fail to look for God in this way.

Faith is what you have in the absence of knowledge... and that absence doesn't bother me because I have got, over the years, a sense of the immense sweep of creation, of the evolutionary process in everything, of how incomprehensible God must necessarily be to be the God of heaven and earth. You can't fit the Almighty into your intellectual categories.

If you want your faith, you have to work for it. It is a gift, but for very few is it a gift given without any demand for time devoted to its cultivation...Even in the life of a Christian, faith rises and falls like the tides of an invisible sea. It's there, even when he can't see it or feel it, if he wants it to be there.

Alice, a friend, recently shared similar thoughts with me:

I grew up believing in a personal God, a God who heard me when I asked him to bless mommy and daddy, my younger brother, and me. I believed God cared for me, would protect me from harm, and loved me even though I sinned. When I prayed, I asked for forgiveness as well as for guidance and blessings.

When I had a struggle with a friend, I asked for God's help. When wondering where to attend college, I sought God's guidance. I also learned to praise him for all he had done for me, for the blessings of friends and family, for food and shelter. Talking to God was a daily necessity for me. I always prayed before going to bed each night.

What would disrupt this lifetime pattern of devotion? What would make me have to reconsider prayer and its meaning in my life?

My relationship with God suddenly was thrown into turmoil. A four-year-old boy I and hundreds of others had been praying for, died. This boy had had a malignant tumor the size of a baseball in the side of his neck. He underwent surgeries, radiation, and severe chemotherapy. I was certain within my spirit that this boy would be cured and live. His cancer never spread. Kids with the same cancer in worse stages had lived. And we had God, whom we trusted to heal him.

In the end, the cancer did not kill him; it was the treatment that weakened his body and immune system so that he was susceptible to a staph infection. The infection caused him to go into septic shock, and after days of being in intensive care he died in my arms. This boy was my son, Daniel.

What good is prayer anyway? This became the ringing question in my mind. I had prayed before for a lot less significant things than the life of a precious child and had seen these petitions answered. But now, how could I ask for anything again when all paled in comparison to the life of my son?

I am still on this journey of seeking. My heart is filled with many emotions. I feel anger at some church groups who make it seem like God can be rubbed like a good-luck charm and will perform in any way the Christian prays. I doubt the sincerity of people who make it seem that because they prayed, God responded as they desired. The focus here is often on the ones who prayed and not on the all-powerful God who answered.

I study the Scriptures on prayer, and the more I read and ponder, the more I wonder if the average Christian really knows much about prayer at all. Perhaps to be in communion with God means to be still before him and meditate on who he is, instead of thinking that prayer is coming to him in a huff with all our requests.

Perhaps for now, prayer for me is looking up in the dark starry night or at the rising sun and pouring forth my simple yet heartfelt words: God, you are there, you are sovereign, you are immortal. I am here, confused, broken, saddened, and extremely mortal. And for your unchanging love, I am thankful.

Though Alice and her husband David held on to the goodness of God after their son's death, there are many for whom such an experience might end with the complete shipwreck of their faith. In a sense, this is not surprising. Sometimes life is like the back of a tapestry where all we can see are the tangled ends on the side facing us, and we must trust that God sees the beauty and purpose on the other.

4.

universality

In all of us there is the need to relate to something or someone greater than ourselves, a striving to elevate our human condition above the daily struggle for survival. There is a yearning for a power that can impart vision, meaning, and purpose to life, provide comfort in times of need, and promise life after death.

Prayer is not the exclusive domain of Christians. Many think that prayer to anyone other than "their" God is idolatry. This attitude is typical of the arrogance with which many western Christians regard the rest of the world. But surely God listens to the longings of all those on earth. As the Psalmist declares, "A broken and contrite heart, O God, you will not despise." We cannot be so narrow-minded that we fail to appreciate God's working in other religions and movements—indeed, in every heart that is open to his spirit.

True, all beliefs are not the same, yet I believe there is something of the divine in every culture, and that every religion thus has something to teach us. The Gospel of John assures us that "the true Light gives light to every person." And if that is so, I should be able to learn something of God from every seeker I meet. Rabbi Kenneth L. Cohen writes, "When religion causes us to forget that other people are created in the divine image, when we are prepared to sacrifice others on the altar of our beliefs, we become fanatics. When we use religion to make God small like ourselves…we are fanatics."

Ever since the beginning of the world, people have believed that turning to a transcendent being would bring blessing and even redemption from their present condition. There was a distinct element of expectancy and acknowledgment of the Supreme Being in the religions of Sumer and Babylon, as well as ancient Egypt. Zoroaster was a Persian prophet who in the sixth century B.C. founded a religion characterized by the worship of an "absolute" God who was engaged in a cosmic fight against evil. The Greek and Roman civilizations, too, as pagan as they may seem today, acknowledged a supreme God. Aboriginal or polytheistic religions such as Hinduism, or pantheistic expressions of spirituality such as those found among Native American tribes, are also centered around the idea of a divine presence, and their notions of petition closely parallel our ideas about prayer.

The need for prayer is recognized in all the major faiths. The believing Jew prays both when he or she is alone, and in the community: in personal prayer he or she is one with the people; the prayers spoken in communion with others are as much personal as they are communal. The Israelites of old were surrounded by a pagan society with its idol worship. Therefore, the important prayer said at the dawn of each new day, the *Shemah*, proclaims the sovereignty of God and the oneness of everything in his creation: "Hear, O Israel: the Lord is our God; the Lord is the only one."

Joe, a doctor I know, finds spiritual truth in the culture and religion of native tribes of the American Southwest. He has a unique view of our communication with God:

Above the earth is a great circle of prayer into which everyone from every faith—and those without faith—can contribute, and from which each can draw strength as well as answers. The beautiful thing is that when you pray, you are connecting with this tremendous power that comes from all corners of the earth.

In Buddhism there is the eightfold path, reminiscent of the Ten Commandments. The goal of detachment from worldly desire is attained through discipline of the senses and devotion to Buddha, who is the manifestation of wisdom and compassion. Silent meditation is valuable, as is "mindfulness," an inner wakefulness to the present moment. Thich Nhat Hanh, a widely respected Zen teacher, writes:

> In a real prayer, you ask only for the things you really need, things that are necessary for your well-being, such as peace, solidity, and freedom—freedom from anger, fear, and craving...You also touch the wholesome seeds in your consciousness and water them. These are seeds of compassion, love, understanding, forgiveness, and joy.

I have many Muslim friends. They have tremendous conviction and depth of faith. My wife and I have also been in the Middle East several times, including Iraq, simply in an attempt to have some small share in the distress of the people there. Warfare and sanctions have caused the deaths of hundreds of thousands of Iraqi children, due to starvation and lack of medical supplies. My heart aches for them. I found it challenging how, in their suffering, many Iraqis are becoming more spiritually attuned and are turning more to prayer. For them and for others the world over, prayer is the only recourse, for it gives them hope and strength to carry on in the face of extreme, unbelievable odds.

A friend who has traveled to Iraq numerous times told me the following story. On one of his visits he had asked an Iraqi what he could do to help the country and its people, and received a most unexpected answer. The man told him to pray for those who have caused the suffering, to pray that when they die, their souls would go to heaven. "Why?" my friend asked. "So they will be comforted for all eternity by the poor children of my country who died by their hands."

Sadly, for many people, prayer has become separated from the acknowledgment of need; that is, rather than being a heartfelt, passionate cry from the heart, it becomes a habit or even an empty ritual. Few things have done more for the demise of living prayer than institutionalized religion. To use the words of an anonymous commentator: "What began as a message in Jerusalem became a philosophy in Greece, a political system in Rome, a culture in Europe, and an enterprise in America."

Though clearly referring to Christianity, the same applies to religions of any brand, as the unique expression of belief given to each person becomes squelched by the powers of conformity, tradition, and structure. Eventually, faith dies away, choked out by the weeds of religiosity and hypocrisy.

According to Pierre Ceresole, "The very minimum demand of any religion worthy of the name is absolute sincerity, not one line more than we really feel and believe. Article number one of our creed must obviously be *truth*." After the First World War, Ceresole founded international work camps in France in the hope that rebuilding would bring about a measure of reconciliation among the nations.

Later, when he was imprisoned for protesting the Nazi regime, he wrote, "To be in prison: here indeed is the one place where religion might be able to make a fresh start at the present time."

Rubén, a Puerto Rican of African-American descent, told me of his long search to find a genuine expression of his faith.

> I went to a really strict school in Brooklyn, St. Augustine's, from the first to the twelfth grade. Then I went to prison for ten years, and although I was a very tough person on the outside, I would cry a lot at night to God. In the back of my head I knew that ultimately he was the only one who could get me out. I mostly stuck around with the politically active crowd, the sports freaks, and the intellectuals, but I really did appreciate the Muslims, the Jews, and the Christians, because I could see that they had a deep foundation inside. The Muslims especially impressed me, because their religion was more than a formality; they had conviction. Nothing was going to distract them from their prayers, no matter what the consequence, even if they were put in the hole, or solitary confinement. Their actions were an expression of a strong faith. The Christians usually played it safe, and their religion was much more of a formality. Sometimes I thought they only prayed when they were kneeling!
>
> On the day I was released from prison the chaplain stood at the doorway—he is a good man—and all he said to me was, "Seek Christians." I wanted to tell him that what I really needed was money, but his comment stuck with me, and I thought a lot about it on my bus ride down to the city. I chewed it over and figured that I'd remember his advice

when things got tough; I'd hang on to it as my "hole card," like in poker. At that point I had been leaning more toward Islam, because of their convictions and the fact that they do more action than talking, but his advice kept going through my mind.

Very quickly I was back onto drugs, and I got real worried, because I knew I would end up in jail again. I knew I would die in jail or get killed on the street. I was kind of down at that point. You know, all my hurts and pains, physically and psychologically and spiritually, were a cry to God, a form of prayer. I knew I had to stop using drugs, but that doesn't mean I gave up selling them (the money was too good). One day I was hanging around in the streets on the Lower East Side, drinking, looking at all the money and the weapons, and I said to myself, "Dear God, I've gotta stop this!" And then I turned to my buddies and said, "You guys, I'm giving all this up." I just knew that I had to change. This was not at all a religious decision, even though I kept talking to God.

I decided to go into a rehab program, but everywhere I went they turned me down; no one wanted to take me. Then I met a guy called Larry who told me to come to the Bowery Mission. He told me all about it. I told him I was not a Christian, and he said that didn't matter. He told me, "If you are on this corner tomorrow that means you want to give it a try." So I was there on the corner the next day.

During my time at the Bowery I learned the Bible really well. I could argue with anybody. Once I was preaching in the chapel, and the place just exploded afterwards, they were so impressed. As I was leaving, an old man said to me, "You can't get to heaven head first." He meant that even if I had all my facts straight, the important thing is that you live what you are preaching. I had to take an inventory of my life. All of us tend to ask for knowledge and wisdom and that is mostly not what we need; we just need to get busy and do what we know is right.

So often we Christians take all the credit and think we "found the Lord" and have done a lot to develop our relationship with God. But mostly it is God who cared about us. He's been leading us and pushing us.

My time at the Bowery Mission was very important, but it was just a first step, "basic training." I prayed that God would lead me to a place where I could be a better person and express my faith without getting too religious about it. I don't ever want to have to tell a person I'm a believer, I want them to see it in me. Our job is to be faithful to the truth we know.

You know, a lot of the people who saved my behind from the grave were whites, and I remember significant things they said during that time that encouraged me to keep going. There was this reverend who told me, "Become a good preacher and then you'll really have to practice it." And John, who said, "I know you're a hardhead, but those are the type of soldiers God wants." Lorraine said, "Rubén, just do good things for other people; don't worry about the rest." Brother Abdul, a Muslim, said, "Just do something for God." Then there was Dave, an orthodox Jew, you know, with a big beard, long curls, a hat, and a long black coat. He would often open up the Torah and tell me stories of people's failings and how God did not give up on them. Years later I realized that when he read those stories to me he was actually praying for me. But perhaps most important was my mother, who prayed incessantly for me. Through all my years in prison and my years on the streets, she never gave up on me, even though I let her down. Her prayers made all the difference. I'll always be thankful for the people God put in my way. They all could easily have said, "To hell with you." But instead they helped and cared and were patient and showed me love. All that was prayer. And, they forgave me. Man, they really had a lot to forgive me for! I owe a lot to all of them.

God always threw something in my way to get my attention. He didn't give up on me. I've heard the story about that famous statue of David, how someone asked Michelangelo how he made such a perfect figure. He answered, "I just kept chipping away all the pieces that weren't David." Well, that is what God has done for me: he just keeps chipping away at the parts of me that aren't really me. And there's this quote from Gandhi that I consider the greatest prayer of all time: "Be the change you want to see." If everyone would do that, this world would be a different place!

But we're still on a journey. Old wounds are still scratched open, like happened once when I was in California and met several old friends from rough times in the past. Things long buried come up to the surface, and you have to deal with it. But I've learned how to cope with these things now, so they don't go back under and fester. You have to stop acting like everything is cool, but be ready to face up when things need dealing with. And there's something else. When I lose sight of God, I hang on to someone who hasn't, so I don't lose the connection. It's something I do. It's an action, it's a prayer. It's a matter of living out the faith.

"What a pity, that so hard on the heels of Christ came the Christians," writes Annie Dillard. Not only have we forgotten Jesus' prayer in John 17, that his disciples may be one even as he and the Father are one; we have divided up his Word and his Body and founded churches instead of being one family of his disciples. In the course of centuries, Christianity has spawned a multitude of divisions, whose outrageous treatment of each other and of different faiths is an insult to his name. More unbelievers have been scared away than converted to the faith.

Whatever our affiliation, each one of us will one day stand alone before God. Then he will not ask: Were you Catholic, Protestant, Muslim, or Jew? but: Did you love your neighbor and feed the hungry? Did you clothe the naked and visit those in prison? So many of us who call ourselves Christians tend to be self-assured and self-righteous; yet all too often our words are not matched by our deeds.

The one overwhelming message that stands at the center of the New Testament is love in action. And we have examples among Christ's followers who, despite human failings, spread the gospel of love. The apostle Paul, who had earlier persecuted the Christians, became one of Christianity's most powerful figures. In his prayers he rarely asks God for those things we most often pray for: safety, physical healing, material blessings. He is more concerned with strength of character, wisdom and discernment, love and sacrifice, personal knowledge of God and spiritual power, courage in spreading the gospel, endurance, and salvation. And unlike many modern Christians, his prayers are not selfish wishes uttered merely on behalf of himself or those dear to him. They are said for the whole earth.

How should we pray? Jesus gives us clear advice. He warns us against false piety and public show, and encourages us to pray privately and simply:

Our Father, who art in heaven,
hallowed be thy name.
Thy kingdom come.
Thy will be done on earth
as it is in heaven.
Give us this day our daily bread.
Forgive us our debts
as we forgive our debtors,
and lead us not into temptation,
but deliver us from evil:
For thine is the kingdom,
the power, and the glory, for ever.

Brief as they are, these twelve lines cover every aspect of human life! Nothing is left out. People recite them many times a day all over the world, mostly heedless of the power and blessing in the words. Through this prayer we enter God's presence, as when Moses approached the burning bush and God said, "Take off your shoes, you are on holy ground."

Thousands of pages have been written about the Lord's Prayer. I believe much of its power lies in its brevity and simplicity. When we have acted in haste or offended the spirit of love, we need to ask for forgiveness. In hours of temptation, we need to ask to be led safely, and we need to be provided for and protected day by day. Above and beyond that, we need the Holy Spirit to fill our hearts and change us from our very foundations. For this to happen we must ask, "Thy will be done." And we must mean it.

5.

god's messengers

As our prayers go up to God, so his spirit comes down to us. Sometimes we may feel a personal response, as though a divine messenger had delivered a specific answer to need. Then there are moments of closeness to God, when we feel palpably carried by his strength, perhaps even by the loving arms of some unearthly being. Such times, though perhaps foreign to the experience of some, are granted more often than we imagine. They do happen.

Whether as messengers, intermediaries, or divine guides that shelter and protect us from danger or temptation, angels are mysterious beings used by God for many purposes. In his Letter to the Colossians, the apostle Paul refers to angels when he says that God created all things "that are in heaven and on earth, visible and invisible, whether thrones or dominions or principalities or powers—all things were created through him and for him."

What else could Paul be referring to when he speaks of invisible powers? Despite widespread interest in angels nowadays, few people seem to take them seriously, or to grasp their significance. They are often dismissed as childish nonsense, even by believers. In contrast, a text from the early church father Origen indicates that the first Christians not only revered angels, but had great confidence in their power as advocates with direct access to the divine:

> When anyone prays, the angels that minister to God and watch over humankind gather round about him and join with him in his prayer. Nor is that all. Every Christian—each of the "little ones" who are in the church—has an angel of his own, who beholds the face of the Father and looks upon the Godhead of the Creator. This angel prays with us and works with us, as far as he can, to obtain the things for which we ask.
>
> "The angel of the Lord," so it is written, "encamps beside those who fear the Lord and delivers them" (Ps. 33:8), while Jacob speaks of "the angel who delivers me from all evils" (Gen. 48:16); and what he says is true not of himself only but of all those who set their trust in God. It would seem, then, that when a number of the faithful meet together genuinely for the glory of Christ, since they all fear the Lord, each of them will have, encamped beside him, his own angel whom God has appointed to guard him and care for him. So, when the saints are assembled, there will be a double church, one of men and one of angels.

In my younger years, I did not give much thought to the presence of angels, though I did not question their existence. I felt sure they were a power to be reckoned with, and in our home they were never talked about lightly. In recent years, however, I have often pondered the words of Jesus: "If only one sinner repents, the angels in heaven will rejoice." That is an amazing statement, and ought to remind us how significant each of us is in God's eyes. The protection people experience each day—often without rational explanation—also points to this.

In the Letter to the Hebrews we are told that angels may come to us in human form. Gillian, an elementary school teacher, once told me the following story:

> Driving home one day, I approached a railroad crossing. There was no barrier, no flashing lights. As my car straddled the rails, it stalled. Then I heard a train coming. When I saw it, I was so terrified that my mind went blank: I could not remember how to restart the car.
>
> Just then a man walked up to me and said simply, "Ma'am, the train is coming." I said, "I know. Thank you." Instantly I knew how to start the car.
>
> I got off the tracks just in time and pulled to the side of the road. Then I looked around to thank the man, but he was nowhere to be seen.

James, a volunteer with the Friends Ambulance Unit in China in 1945, had a similar experience.

> I was assigned to a medical team in Tengchung, near the Burma border, and was asked to go to Kunming, about five hundred miles east, to get medical supplies and equipment. After negotiating a ride for the first two hundred miles (to the city of Bao Shan) with the Chinese Army, I started off with Yang Yung Lo, a Chinese volunteer who could not speak English.
>
> On our return trip we were dropped off at Bao Shan, where we hoped a U.S. Army convoy would pick us up and take us back to Tengchung. After two days of waiting, we were informed that a convoy was on its way, but that we would have to meet it on the other side of the river where we were waiting.
>
> Yang Yung Lo and I were desperate. The river was only about fifty feet wide, but we had half a ton of medical supplies with us, and the bridge, which had many boards missing, was slippery and unsafe for trucks.

Just then a Chinese man (or so he seemed) appeared. He was dressed in white. He asked us who we were and what we were doing. I told him we were with the Red Cross and were trying to transport medical supplies across the bridge. He understood immediately and said, "I will help you." I don't remember the details, but we made many trips across the bridge, and all went very smoothly. Afterward I went to thank our helper. He had disappeared.

It wasn't until later, when we were safely on our way with the convoy, that I realized how our spirits had been lifted the moment the stranger appeared on the scene, and that we had understood each other without difficulty, despite the language barrier. I have thought of the experience often since. I do not understand it, but I am certain that God's hand was in it.

Johann Christoph Blumhardt, a nineteenth-century pastor well known in his native Germany, experienced the intervention of angels on numerous occasions. Once a small child in his parish was running down a village street when an ox-drawn farm wagon, loaded with manure, rumbled toward him. Passersby shouted at the driver, but it was too late. The boy was knocked down and a heavy wheel ran right over his chest. Seconds later, to the amazement of onlookers, the boy was on his feet again, unhurt. Asked if he was all right, the boy looked at them in surprise. "Yes. Didn't you see the man lift the wheel?"

Another time, at a train station, Blumhardt was so intent on the newspaper he was reading that he walked right off the end of the platform. Instead of falling, though, he felt himself supported as if by invisible arms and gently set on the ground. He did not speak about this to anyone but his immediate family; he accepted it quietly, like a child, and thanked

God for protecting him. To the modern mind, the incident seems uncanny. To the believer, it simply fulfills the well-known promise in Psalm 91: "He will give his angels charge of you to guard you in all your ways. On their hands they will bear you up, lest you dash your foot against a stone."

I sometimes wonder how many more prayers would be answered if we prayed more earnestly and with greater reverence for the mysteries of the unseen angel world. I say "angel world" in the sense that angels, as messengers of God, are invested with divine authority, which I believe they carry with them when they come down to us humans.

Ulrich and Ellen, close friends of mine over many decades (Ellen was my secretary), experienced this in a very real way. They had eight children, but lost their two youngest in the same year, 1977. The first, Mark John, died at age three-and-a-half from cancer; I have told his story at length in my book *A Little Child Shall Lead Them*. Five months after this death, Ellen herself almost died.

During the birth of their youngest child, Marie Johanna, Ellen bled so heavily that she required full resuscitation and transfusion. Sufficient blood was not available and members of her community with the right type had to be awakened at night and asked to donate. Within an hour, new blood was circulating through her body. Yet still the outlook was bleak, and the attending physician commented, "All that will help now is prayer." Sensing the same, those of us gathered at the hospital, including those who had just donated their blood, interceded in earnest prayer. Ellen did survive, with all her faculties intact, but Marie Johanna suffered brain damage from lack of oxygen during the birth.

Because the doctors at the university hospital felt medicine had nothing more to offer, the baby was brought home. She lived for nine more weeks.

My father, Ulrich and Ellen's pastor at the time, said repeatedly during those days, "Marie's life is on a thread between heaven and earth. Only prayer is keeping her alive." Indeed, the baby's doctors said her survival was beyond reason—more than science could account for.

Then, on the day before Christmas, she died. Her mother remembers:

> On Christmas Eve we were gathered around our baby. I was holding her when suddenly Marie, who had never focused her eyes on anything before, opened them wide—they were like oceans: deep, dark blue, and bright—and she was looking at something.
>
> There was a movement, a breath of air. I felt Marie's soul lifted from my arms and pass in front of me, and firm, stiff wings brushed my face. There was a scent, like the fragrance of a garden. Our children sensed that something had happened. I knew. We looked down and could see that she was gone.

The presence of angels remains a mystery: completely real, but not completely recognized or acknowledged. Yet precisely at the point beyond which our minds cannot comprehend, we must allow our hearts to believe. A mother recently related the following to me:

> One afternoon my little daughter Jane and I were sitting by an open window in our third-floor apartment. She was in her highchair and I was feeding her cereal. I left the room for a moment to get milk from the fridge, and when I returned my heart skipped a beat: Jane was not only standing for the first time in her life, but she had turned

around and was leaning out the window. I didn't make a sound—afraid that if I shouted she would lose her balance and fall. I moved across the room and grabbed her from behind. Relief flooded over me as I held her in my arms. Then I looked down from the window and saw, some thirty feet below, my neighbor Cynthia. She was standing there, looking up, not saying a word, with her arms wide open, ready to catch Jane. I thanked God silently, hugged Jane, and wept.

Later I went to thank Cynthia, but she had no memory of the incident; in fact, she claimed she was never there.

Carole, a close friend who died after a three-year battle with cancer, wrote to me regarding angels:

For some reason anything about angels goes straight to the heart. We don't know how many there are, what they look like, all the people they must be protecting every day, or the comfort they bring. It is hard to conceive of God being everywhere, listening to every heart at every moment, and it's hard to imagine him even wanting to hear us, so small, insignificant, and completely unworthy as we are. Somehow angels seem to be his fingers, his arms, his heart. To think of this makes it possible to let the fear drop (or at least slowly go away) and to feel carried by something far greater than it is ever possible to describe. In the past I always shut out the whole idea of angels, but in this past month they have suddenly become real to me. God sends his messengers of comfort every day, every hour, to take the fear and bleakness out of dying.

6.

emotional
suffering

Twenty-five-year-old Rachel was an energetic and
enthusiastic kindergarten teacher, when she was suddenly
overcome by depressive thoughts and intense feelings of
worthlessness. This progressed to delusional thoughts and
bizarre behavior and speech, as well as attempts at suicide.
Rachel was counseled, given both medical and spiritual
support, and hospitalized. A few weeks later, she was dis-
charged, although it was almost a year before she felt she
was herself again. Significantly, throughout this whole epi-
sode, she insisted, even when she was delusional, that she
was not going to be a mental patient. Her determination was
amazing. Eventually Rachel recovered completely; she was
able to discontinue all medications and resume a full-time
job, and she has had no relapse. In her own words:

> I had always enjoyed working hard and being with chil-
> dren, but I gradually became more and more exhausted. I
> couldn't seem to cope with my work, and at night I could
> not sleep.
>
> I was admitted to the psych ward on my birthday. I was
> desperate, and I remember thinking that this would be my
> last birthday—I was so sure I was going to die. But then I

began to meet other patients, people who were suffering much more than I was, and that helped me to get my mind off myself. I tried to keep busy, no matter how rotten I felt. I made myself get up and do things. I even practiced my flute.

I'll never forget how abnormal I still felt when I came home. I could not stick to anything for any length of time, because one of the anti-depressants made me very restless. I cried a lot and prayed a lot. I felt defeated one moment and angry the next, but I knew I would be able to come off all my medications eventually because I had never needed them before.

I can never be grateful enough that I was freed from the demon of that depression. For it was more than determination that pulled me through: I experienced a freeing. People were praying for it and God was there too, though at times it seemed like he was very far away. But I am also thankful that I went through this difficult time. It might sound crazy, but it has given me a new outlook on life. Now, when people are sick, I know what they are going through, and I can relate to those who are suffering. I know what people mean when they say, "You can't do anything in your own strength."

Despite our culture's reputation for tolerance, there is still a stigma attached to suicide. Even as a topic of conversation, it largely remains taboo. Most people are reluctant to speak about death, and when it comes to suicide, they tend to avoid it altogether.

No death is more distressing than suicide, and it is frightening when a person seriously contemplates such a step. The prophet Jeremiah reminds us: "A man's life is not his own; it is not for man to direct his steps." Christianity has condemned suicide for a similar reason: because it negates the possibility of redemption. Suicide says, "I'm beyond hope — my problems are too big even for God to handle." It denies that God's grace is greater than our weakness. While such a view may seem understandable, it is deceptive because it leads a person to believe that death will end the inner pain, when in reality it is pain's ultimate infliction. C.S. Lewis wrote the following to a friend who had recently lost his wife and in his anguish considered suicide so that they might be reunited again:

> She was further on than you, and she can help you more where she is now than she could have done on earth. You must go on. That is one of the many reasons why suicide is out of the question. Another is the absence of any ground for believing that death *by that route* would reunite you with her. Why should it? You might be digging an eternally unbridgeable chasm. Disobedience is not the way to get nearer to the obedient.

Kaye, a woman who wrote to me from California after reading an article I wrote on suicide, lost a sister through suicide, and almost took her own life, too—three times. When still an infant, she was almost killed by her mother; later she suffered sexual abuse at the hands of a man she trusted.

> For those of us who survive the ravages of suicide and learn from our experiences, abundant life is in store. We do not live lives that are lies. And the shards of what was can be molded into beautiful pottery. I speak for those who have experienced "the dark night of the soul" as I have, and have survived to tell about it.
>
> I believed in God through every moment of my long, dark struggle, and he is the reason I am alive today. I listened to his voice that night when he said: "Don't do it.

Don't commit suicide." So although I had the syringe full of deadly drugs at my side, I did not do it. I obeyed God and am very grateful today that I did. But I was angry, very angry that I had to live in hell three more years...

We who are (or were) suicidal live with shattered spirits and souls. To exist with a shattered soul is excruciatingly painful because we live by going through the motions. We know there is more there, but we are trapped as if in a giant ice cube...

Depression is a sickness of the soul starved for unconditional love – the unconditional love that only God can provide. All people have their dark side, and our love is only conditional; that's why we need God. He knows us better than we know ourselves, and he is still the Great Healer. He has promised us trouble in life, but he has also promised us joy and peace in the midst of our trouble and grief.

Yes, prayer is the best help for despair and for suicidally depressed people. At times, eating – or even just breathing – is the only prayer they can pray. But God understands that this is enough of a prayer!

However poor and inadequate prayer may be, it is the only real help for despair. Even if we think we don't know how to pray, we can turn to God. Praying with the psalms can be a help, since the psalmist often shares our innermost longing and voices it in prayer: "Give ear to my words, O Lord, consider my sighing," and "In my anguish I cried to the Lord, and he answered by setting me free." Prayer can be a mainstay, even when we despair to the point of entertaining suicidal thoughts, or when God seems far away. Jane Kenyon writes:

My belief in God, especially the idea that a believer is part of the body of Christ, has kept me from harming myself.

When I was in so much pain that I didn't want to be awake or aware, I've thought to myself, If you injure yourself, you're injuring the body of Christ, and Christ has been injured enough.

In *The Adolescent,* Dostoyevsky emphasizes the importance of praying for those who are desperate.

"How do you look upon the sin of suicide," I asked Makar...

"Suicide is man's greatest sin," he said with a sigh, "but God alone can judge it, for only God knows what and how much a man can bear. As for us, we must pray tirelessly for the sinner. Whenever you hear of that sin, pray hard for the sinner, at least sigh for him as you turn to God, even if you never knew him—that will make your prayer all the more effective."

"But would my prayer be of any help to him since he's already condemned?"

"Who can tell? There are many—oh, so many!—people without faith who just confuse the ignorant. Don't listen to them because they themselves don't know where they're going. A prayer for a condemned man from a man still alive will reach God, and that's the truth. Just think of the plight of a man who has no one to pray for him. And so, when you pray in the evening before going to sleep, add at the end, 'Lord Jesus, have mercy on all those who have no one to pray for them.' This prayer will be heard and it will please the Lord. Also pray for all the sinners who are still alive: 'O Lord, who holdest all destinies in thy hand, save all the unrepentant sinners.' That's also a good prayer."

As my father wrote in his book *Discipleship:* "It is a great mistake to think that we can understand our own hearts. We may understand ourselves superficially, but only God really knows our hearts. Therefore, even if we suffer the severest temptations, trials, and attacks from the Evil One, we can always turn to God with trust and great hopes for victory."

If prayer fails to comfort a suicidal person, we who are close to him must have faith and believe for him. When someone sinks in darkness and thinks he is separated from God, he must be assured that others will pray for him. There is profound protection in the prayers of others.

Much of the emotional isolation in modern society is rooted in our confusion about the real purpose in living: we forget that our first task is to love God with all our heart and soul, and to love our neighbor as ourselves. If we took these two great commandments seriously, much loneliness and depression could be averted. Loving our neighbor is prayer in action, and it is something each of us can do. I often wonder whether we do not rely too heavily on experts. When a person is desperate and suicidal, an "expert" may be the last person he wants to face: after all, who can cope with analysis or advice when he feels unable even to face himself? Naturally one cannot rule out the use of psychiatry or medication, but we should not forget that often the simple support of a listening ear—a friend or family member, pastor or priest—is the best help.

Here is part of a letter I received recently from a mother of three children:

> I was admitted to a psychiatry ward twice, the second time because of severe depression after the birth of my son. In a sense, hospitalization removed me from the stressful situation, and I felt that the personnel there accepted me as I was and did not expect things of me that I felt unable to do. But long-term help did not come from hospitalization or

medication. It came through the prayers and love of family and friends.

In dealing with someone with mental illness, I think understanding and accepting that person is the best help. I didn't find it easy when someone said to me at that time, "We all have our down days." It made me feel she didn't understand it at all, and I felt she expected me to somehow pull myself out of this depression, which I simply could not do. You see, I had no control over how I felt at that time after the birth. I couldn't laugh, couldn't cry, didn't feel any love for my baby or my husband. It was hell, I tell you. I felt cut off from God and man.

Basically I couldn't function. I spent most of my days on my bed. My mother did a lot for our baby and for me. I felt incapable of doing anything. And that is hard for people to understand; maybe they thought I was just lazy. But slowly I recovered. I was able to do more, work again gradually, as I got better.

People didn't really know how to help, although they tried. But my minister understood. Whenever I told him I couldn't pray – and that was a real need for me – he always answered, "Then I will pray for you." And that comforted me.

I am thankful for all the prayers that were said for me when I could see no light at the end of the tunnel. More than that, I am grateful for the sensitivity toward my situation shown by those near to me. That was a real form of intercession. For a long time I believed I would never know joy again, that I would be trapped in this horrible snare of depression forever. But my husband and my friends believed for me and prayed for me, and I came through.

There have always been people who suffered the ravages of mental illness – depressive thoughts, manic tendencies,

emotional instability, overwhelming anxieties, and delusional ideas. It is those who suffer from this last imbalance
who most often receive the cold shoulder, perhaps because
we see in them our own instability and recoil from the
uncomfortable suspicion that we, too, have the potential to
become unwired.

Some psychotic or schizophrenic people suffer in a way
not unlike the demonic possession described in the New
Testament. Those people were drawn to Jesus as to a mag-
net. Indeed, they seemed to recognize the Son of God more
clearly than other, apparently healthy, persons.

Elisabeth, an acquaintance who died recently, was born
in Germany during the Nazi years. Forced to leave Europe
with her family as a young girl, she ended up in England,
but there was no possibility of long-term refuge. Elisabeth's
father was interned in a camp for German aliens and then
sent to a prison in Canada. As for the family, they were
forced to emigrate again, this time to South America.

All this turmoil affected Elisabeth. Her lively and origi-
nal personality gave way to unusual behavior and eventually to overt schizophrenia. Because of her illness, Elisabeth
and those close to her lived in continuous exhaustion as one
wave after another of distress, spiritual torment, mental
anguish, or physical suffering engulfed her. Often it felt as
if powerful forces were binding her, and prayer was the only
thing that could calm her.

In her last years, standard psychiatric help and countless
medications were of no use. Only love and the emotional
support of those around her seemed to help. Singing and
praying brought her through the roughest hours, and again
and again she found inner peace, even if only temporarily.

Remembering Elisabeth, I often wonder whether those whom we think of as emotionally unbalanced are perhaps a much greater gift to us than we realize and dare to admit. They are vulnerable, and they are poor in spirit. Through them, if we allow it, a part of the gospel becomes a reality that is otherwise closed to us. The apostle Paul tells us to carry each other's burdens. What does this mean, other than supporting one another, loving one another, and praying for one another? Let us never forget, too, that in the gospels Jesus is called the Great Healer. He did not come for the healthy, but for the sick.

7.

illness

Adversity can come in many forms, including poverty and persecution. But when it takes the shape of illness, even the most self-possessed person may find himself turning to God for help. Like nothing else, the physical pain of illness makes us realize the limitations of our human strength and abilities. Unlike health and happiness, it teaches us to pray.

Paul and Nadine, a young couple I know, were looking forward to the arrival of their first child. Barry came, healthy and beautiful, but within a few days it became evident that all was not right, and he was transferred to nearby Yale University Hospital for evaluation.

The same week, an older woman in their church died, someone they knew and loved. During the funeral service, Nadine was suddenly gripped by a premonition: our child will be the next one we will be burying. Paul remembers:

> Right after the funeral, we got a phone call from Yale: we were to come immediately because our son was much worse. The diagnosis had been made: Barry had a metabolic defect, a genetic derangement of his body chemistry. Worse, nothing could be done. The diagnosis had been made too late to save him, and his brain was already damaged.

The people in the ICU did their best, but Barry just kept getting worse. We wanted to bring him home to die, but the doctors wouldn't permit it. That was very hard for us.

In the night Barry deteriorated further. He was still conscious, but it was clear he was dying. Finally we asked if we could take him to a quiet room, away from all the machines and tubes and wires, and we were allowed to do this. We held him in our arms and, with several people from our church, we prayed together and sang with him for at least an hour, until he died.

Because Barry's condition was genetic, we have had to evaluate each of our children who followed him; and with each pregnancy we have had to put our trust in God completely, preparing for what may be found. But we have worried too much, I think, and that never helps. All we can do as parents is to ask God to protect our children every day. And we must believe that he will do this.

Another couple I know, John and Tessy, also experienced a sudden shattering of the bliss that followed the arrival of their first child. John writes:

Like many firstborns, Lakesha's delivery was long and difficult for her mother, but we were overjoyed by her apparent healthiness.

What no one knew was that our little one had a serious deformity in her heart: the two biggest blood vessels in the body were switched over at the point where they attached to the heart. This meant that the oxygenated blood was going in a circle between her lungs and half of the heart, and the blood from the rest of the body was being pumped right back out again, without going to the lungs.

Lakesha was only being kept alive through a very small artery that functions during fetal life, but usually disappears within the first weeks of life outside the womb. Soon she became pale, and one day we were rushing to the hospital with a "blue baby;" there, catheter surgery was performed to keep her alive at least for the time being.

In 1988 there were only three places in the world that would correct Lakesha's potentially fatal heart problem: London, Boston, and Philadelphia. We decided on Philadelphia.

At this point I must say that our hopes for a successful operation were sobered by the death of our neighbor's first child, who was born just three days after our little girl and died a week later. It was a stark reminder of the fragility of life.

In Philadelphia we were received personally by the surgeon and staff at Children's Hospital. Despite the hi-tech atmosphere of the place we felt the loving concern of everyone involved. Allowing our baby to disappear through the doors of the operating suite was a test of our trust in God. During the surgery we waited in the hall with people from Norway, Israel, California, Texas, and Australia, all there to have their children's heart defects corrected. Those hours of waiting stretched on forever, and we were irritable and nervous, our emotions strained. In the next days we were allowed only short visits to the ICU, and it was difficult to see any signs of life at all in our daughter.

Then a child at the hospital who was there for the same operation as Lakesha died. After that we heard news from home that the wife of a close friend had suddenly died of cancer. Sometimes our senses seemed heightened; at other times we felt numb. But beyond our words and feelings was the growing realization that all life is in God's hands.

We received many encouraging letters during this ordeal, but one stands out in my mind because it was written with such warmth and sincerity. Harry Taylor, a frail old man who knew my wife when she was a child, wrote from

England: "Of one thing we are certain: God hears our prayers for your daughter's healing. His will is always love, here among us and also eternally."

Lakesha survived, and she is now a healthy young woman.

Tom, a physician who has practiced neurology for some thirty years, notes the importance of prayer in the face of medical difficulties:

In my office, we see so many people who have emotional needs, who have no background of prayer or hope. And for those people we have to pray that somehow God will guide us in helping them to see that there is more to their problem than just the physical. There's an emotional and, more importantly, a spiritual aspect. When we can no longer provide physical relief, then we must try to impart spiritual help. And sometimes, all we can do at that point is pray for them and, in rare instances, pray with them. Prayer sometimes opens up a whole new venue to these people, which they had never known before.

There are also times when we're doing everything that is medically possible, and still there is the inevitable – that over the next couple of weeks the patient will probably die. Then I tell the patient and his family that they need to make the most of what is left of life, but even more, they really have to start looking to and understanding the great and larger picture of what life is all about. And that kind of thing requires us to talk about a belief in God, and to say at that point that we have transcended what medicine can do, and now our hope has to be in something other than the physician and in something other than ourselves.

It also happens at the opposite end, that the path we've pursued has not been correct with regard to the diagnosis or the therapy. Then it becomes the task of the physician to pray; he has to start looking beyond himself to God, asking for help and guidance in what he's doing. And sometimes he must ask for forgiveness.

I often find that when you tell a patient there is nothing you can do, through no fault of your own, the patient becomes angry — not only at the physician, but angry at everybody. Then I will frequently sit down and talk, not about physical things, but spiritual things. Because at such a time, when a patient is dying, the family and the patient start to understand the whimsical and fleeting nature of life. It's an opportunity for a physician to be a better physician. We are no longer dealing with biochemistry, physiology, anatomy. We're dealing with an area of medicine we don't understand, but an area that can truly give the patient more comfort, more hope, than we could give ourselves.

It's a leap of faith at that point, and we have to help the patient make that leap. We have to say, "Look, there's nothing we can do medically, but there are other things that can be done."

There are times when serious illness or tragedy strikes so forcefully that one hardly dares to ask God for what might seem an impossible reversal of fate. In such an hour, our relationship with God takes on a rare and unforgettable intensity. A friend, Jonathan, recalls such an incident:

I remember one night when I was a third- or fourth-year medical student. I was working in the emergency room, and in came a man who had just had a horrible mining accident. His head was crushed: blood and tissue and fluid were everywhere, and yet he was still alive, his heart was still going. The emergency crew came swooping in, ten or twenty people with machines and electricity and everything. I was standing on the side.

Then Rod, our neurosurgeon, pushed them all aside and pulled a curtain right around the patient, beckoning me in. He put his arm around me and said, "Now is a time when we are thankful we believe." That's all he said. And he put his hand on that man's shoulder, and the two of us just stood there silently until the man stopped breathing. Tears were coming down my face. I was totally shaken up; I had never seen anything so traumatic before. I looked at Rod, and tears were pouring down his face. And behind the curtain were all these professionals who thought they could save this man. I've never forgotten it. There are times when you must simply stop and let God take charge.

I experienced something similar in the death of Fritz, a man I knew as a child in South America. Fritz came to the Bruderhof in 1927, drawn by its radical social outlook and its practice of total community. He had just completed a rigorous blacksmith's apprenticeship, but was also skilled in other areas of manual labor, including building. He considered himself a member of the "true proletariat" and was a convinced Socialist, disillusioned with the churches and with previous political involvements. Fritz hoped that something new would come from within the labor movement.

At the end of that year, death came unexpectedly to the little community. A one-year-old child died of smoke inhalation when green wood was used to stoke the stove in the room where she lay sleeping. Fritz, who previously had thought little of religion, was deeply shaken; in fact, the incident brought about his first real turning to faith.

Twenty years later, at the end of 1947, Fritz was working on a lathe, turning a large ring-like base for a Christmas wreath. Suddenly the wood cracked and the ring broke loose, spinning upward and striking Fritz on the forehead, just above the right eye.

My great-aunt Monika, a nurse, arrived at the scene very quickly and found the injury to be large and deep. She bandaged it to stop the bleeding, but soon Fritz began to vomit. Later, at the community's small mission hospital, an examination revealed that he had suffered a depressed skull fracture. Apart from cleansing the wound and stitching it, nothing could be done. Fritz's condition was critical and he was in great pain, yet he was still able to sing Christmas carols with those who gathered around his bed. The next day he developed a high fever. Two days later he became unconscious.

Four nights after the accident, Fritz's condition began to deteriorate rapidly. Paralysis had started on the left side and soon progressed to the other side. There were blood clots in the largest vessels of the brain, and copious pus. A prayer meeting was called at 5:45 A.M. and earnest appeals were made to God to save Fritz.

As if things weren't difficult enough, outward circumstances in the community put great strain on the small medical staff and made the situation even harder. The same night, a child at the hospital required an emergency tracheotomy; hours later my wife's mother, Margrit, gave birth to her eleventh child. Throughout the hospital, meanwhile, other patients were groaning in their suffering.

Several times during the next day, friends and relatives met to intercede for Fritz, and that evening they gathered to pray and read from the New Testament. Then they went to sing outside his window. The songs were a true communal prayer – the words fitting the need of the hour, and the music an expression of unity and of the longing that everything be done in harmony with God's will.

Fritz died during the singing. Everyone stood there for a long time in silence. Fritz was a vigorous, strong man, forty-two years old—and now he was gone, leaving a wife and six children. The grief was overwhelming, and so was the renewed realization of man's smallness and frailty.

Life changed overnight for William and Barbara, a couple I have known for years, when their four-year-old daughter was diagnosed with Type I diabetes. Without daily insulin injections, careful monitoring, and a strictly controlled diet, her blood sugar levels would go too high or too low, which could lead to seizures or loss of consciousness or even death. It's a twenty-four-hour a day job with no vacations. Four year later Barbara wrote:

> What do we want for our daughter? What do we pray for? Our prayer for her is not that different from what we wish for each of our children: that she can lead as carefree and as selfless a life as possible.
>
> We have trust that God can do all things, and that he can heal her if it is his will. We have thought about this over the past years but have never ourselves prayed for complete healing for her, though it is not in any sense of unbelief. We do not question why our daughter has this condition. But we do know that God speaks to us through her and through her disease.
>
> If some child on earth needs to be burdened with a medical disorder, we would prefer that it is our child rather than a child in a Third-World country. We have availability of medical care, a caring community around us, and a sup-

portive church. As for our daughter, she has trust in God's plans for the future. She is certain that when God's kingdom comes, she will be cured.

Healing can take place in different ways, not always in the form we imagine and hope for. There is physical healing, and there is also inner healing—freedom or relief from fear of the unknown and fear of death. Sometimes neither seems to be given us. Ultimately, though, our prayer must be that whatever happens, God's will is done, not ours.

Dale and Carole had been married more than twenty years. Carole had battled depression most of her life, and although medications were helpful, she and Dale went through many hard times together.

Then Carole was diagnosed with breast cancer. It was a fairly aggressive type, but it was caught early and had not spread too far, so the outlook was good. Although Carole's specialists thought surgery alone would be sufficient, she was keen to go through chemotherapy as well. So she underwent the painful and disfiguring surgery, and then bravely proceeded through chemotherapy, a dose every two weeks for six months.

Carole was granted a complete remission for the next two years. However, she then began to have chest and bone pain, and an X-ray showed a spread of the cancer to her lungs. Carole's outlook, even with further therapy, was very poor. But she was not one to give up easily. Though she declined further chemotherapy, her attitude more than made up for that. What she faced is something to be envied: eternity. It is something each one of us faces every day, whether we realize it or not, because none of us knows when death will come. One of the most valuable lessons we can ever learn is that life is meaningful only in the context of eternity.

Carole was well aware that she might not live long. Her prayer was simply to become an instrument for God. In the Bible, James describes a special prayer ceremony that involves the laying of hands on a person who is ill. This is a specific calling upon God, an earnest pleading for his power to be made manifest in the sick person. When I asked Carole if she wanted the church to intercede for her in this way, she wrote:

> I have always kind of steered away from that, because it seemed like it is prayer for God to heal *if* it's his will, and I cannot imagine healing and wholeness *not* being God's will for anyone. But I don't know how that fits into God's plan, because death and suffering do happen and it has often been a vehicle to bring other things to pass. I would really appreciate the prayer with hands laid on me, if it could be done in the sense that I find new courage and joy and peace. I do not want to be the focus of attention. There is such a tremendous struggle going on in so many places all over the world, and so many other people are sick and dying, so really I would like it to be a laying on of hands for all the suffering people in the world.

Later Carole wrote to my wife:

> As I understand it, my cancer is already quite widespread, which Dale and I have suspected for quite a while. If chemotherapy gives only a small chance of recovery, we don't want to sacrifice the last months of my life with days and nights vomiting and being totally out of it. It is not an easy decision. We all want to "do something." But perhaps the best thing may be simply to look to God for strength, peace,

and courage to face whatever comes, which we want to do in any case. You know, my faith is a bit like a damp dishrag. I don't have any question that God can heal…I never read in the gospels that Jesus said, "I don't want to heal you." But I don't—and can't—have any idea how God plans our lives. The only thing we know for sure is that Dale and I want our lives to be in God's hands. And whatever form that takes, we are not only willing but eager, with heart and soul, for that to happen.

I really must witness to the power of prayer. My whole life has been one tremendous fight against depression, against suicide, and I even had to be kept under strict watch at times. There were also times when my spirits were very high and I was unpredictable. The members of our church have prayed for me continuously, even when I had no courage whatsoever to even go to worship meetings, and in these last years I've also been faced with the fight against cancer. All I can say is that for me the battle was won five years ago when tremendous victory was given over my mental illness—when the darkness of depression had been so thick that I could even visualize death. This is completely gone now, and it is making my fight against cancer much easier. No one should feel sorry for me, because I can only say I have tremendous joy, and what I experience now in my fight with cancer is nothing compared to that fight against depression and suicide years ago.

Over the last year of her life, Carole was continually in our prayers. She still had her ups and downs and shared them openly, not only with my wife and me, but also with other members of our congregation. A few months before she died, she wrote to me again:

With a free and very relieved heart, Dale and I want to stop the whole medical process now, even if the cancer has spread to my liver. Medically there is really no chance for me, and to go into heavy-duty chemo next week would just be the end of things. I don't want to waste any more time in that way. None of us knows what God has in mind for us, be it life or *Life,* and with or without chemo, all we want is God's will for us. What means so very much to me in these days is to be up and around, working when I can, and to be in constant contact with young people, people who are enthusiastic for life. All of that will not be possible if we undergo another round of chemotherapy.

Just to say again — we have not been able to, or even wanted to, ask for healing in our personal prayers. This doesn't come out of any "holy" conviction, but it's just that we feel deeply that God's will *is* going to be done, with or without medicine.

And in another letter:

I just want to tell you that these last few years have been the happiest of my whole life, in spite of the cancer. I've always been so frantically afraid of death, and now I'm just waiting for it, whenever it happens. Dale and I have both been given this indescribable gift — the prayer of the church. I don't think in all our lives we have experienced so much peace and happiness and very deep joy. It's just a wonder to us both. The physical pain is sometimes hard to bear, but even that is relieved, knowing that help and prayer are always there.

We've talked together about dying many, many times. Dale said that the time when he really faced losing me was when I went into the lock-up ward during a bout with depression. He said he feared I would never be able to "come back," and now we're so very much more together, even though we've had a few rough patches since then, but who hasn't?

Dale and I feel that we need to really make use of the days and the minutes we have left together. We have often talked about how we wasted probably *years* of our lives with grudges and things we couldn't work out, or we had trouble in our marriage because we couldn't find humility with one another. We cannot change those things now, so we just have to keep making a new beginning every day.

My death will not be easy for Dale, but because of the togetherness we feel, it is also a tremendous comfort for us both that we have each other in our hearts. We love the talk and laughter of the young people in the evenings. Conversation and laughter are such precious things, and so encouraging to one in my situation.

If we always think, well, maybe tomorrow we'll do this, or tomorrow I'll follow through on that, it doesn't make sense. We actually don't have tomorrow. None of us has tomorrow. We only have today and we only have each other, the person sitting next to us, the person we work with. That's a tremendous challenge to me – to really make use of every minute we have.

To Carole, making every minute count simply meant thinking of others. But that was no mere cliché. Thinking of the loneliness Dale would suffer after she was gone, she told him more than once that she hoped he would remarry, and even suggested Ida, a close friend who was raising an adopted child on her own. Ida had prayed repeatedly for a husband, and a father for her child, over many years. As Carole explained in one of her last letters to my wife and me:

> I know this may seem strange or unusual, but I have given Dale my wedding ring. I cannot see putting it in a grave. I want it to be used again. I want him to remarry, and we have talked openly about this. It is a mystery, something I hardly

understand — giving Dale up and yet feeling so very close to him. But it is also a joy to be able to be so completely open and honest with one another. People say love will "find the way," and we've reminded each other of this too. It's so true. I am sure that if we really live and die in God's will, our hearts will be together forever.

Following Carole's death, a friendship did in fact develop between Dale and Ida, and then a deep love. After some time Dale proposed, and they are now married.

8.

despair

No matter how remote God sometimes seems, I believe
he is never far away. Like the angel who stood with the
Hebrew youths in the fiery furnace, he is always there—
Emmanuel, God with us. He joins us in our pain. But what
can we say to the despairing person who feels that God does
not hear her cries?

Janine, an acquaintance, sent me the following thoughts
during a time of turmoil in her family:

> Our four kids are in their bumpy teen years. It is stressful
> as we try to balance the freedom we want to give them as
> they grow into young adults with the guidance we know
> they need. Just the regular parent-teen thing, you know.
> But my husband seems to take it all a bit harder than nor-
> mal. As the conflicts seem to escalate, his resolve weakens.
> The kids, insecure, push him further, asking for—yet chal-
> lenging—each boundary.
>
> A terrifying event many years ago, when our lives were
> physically threatened, still shakes my husband badly and
> haunts him. Moving from our home of twenty-five years,
> and taking a new job for the first time in many years, adds
> tension. His emotional stability corrodes, and he succumbs.
>
> This is depression with a capital D. Not discouragement,
> not just a state of being down, or sad, or low. Depressed:

numb, absent, flat, grey, gone. For me, it's a matter of living with someone who is no longer the same person I married: where are you, my husband? Blank.

Our sons react, not comprehending. My daughter grows quiet and turns inward, confused. I am angry, then frustrated, then stoic. Meanwhile, as days become weeks, my husband's depression drags on, and his self-confidence trickles away. We pray each day, asking for help. We attend worship and prayer services at our local church, hoping things will improve. Some weeks are better. Sometimes even a few months go by and everything seems okay.

When there are bad days, I just tell myself to hang in there. After all, I've always been the optimistic, organized, have-it-all-together type. Then my husband goes into another tailspin and drowns in a new sea of depression. I am stranded, left to face the doubled darkness and the pummeling waves alone.

I pray. More often than before, and more earnestly than ever. Lord, help me! Help my husband! Help my children! I pray.

But months pass, and our family goes from bad to worse. Our daughter grows quieter and quieter. Our sons become rebellious, dishonest, estranged from us. When I catch one of them lying to me, my adrenaline rushes. I'm so angry I don't know what to do. I try to be loving, but firm. My husband just stands there, silent, the depression crashing in over him again. My heart feels scorched, but I harden myself, determined to fight with all I've got.

My husband loses more ground and tries to compensate for his feelings of parental failure by giving in to every whim of the children in an effort to win their love. When my sons continue to rebel, my husband even takes their side, separating himself from me. We go round and round, up and down. I feel like so many windows of our marriage have shattered, it is impossible to walk between the shards. What to sweep out? What to repair? I want to scream, I want to run, but I can't. I don't.

People say, "I'll pray for you." Or, "Just pray." They're right. But sometimes those phrases get bloated with the promise of magic—abracadabra—and then it's twice as hard when they disperse, empty, into thin air. Of course, I go on praying anyway, all the time, unceasingly, as the Bible says. Like the widow, I bang on the judge's door every day so that God will tire of me and answer in exasperation. I pray during the long sleepless nights. I fast, many times, secretly, so my Father will repay in secret. Tears flow in place of words, for God knows my need better than I do. I ask. I seek. I knock. I shout, because God is so far away, and I want to make him hear me!

I begin to get migraine headaches, which isn't as bad as the constant searing pain in the spinal-cord area of my back. I agonize, day after day, for my family. In between I try to live. I see suffering all over the world—unbelievable chaos and death. My own needs shrink in comparison.

I begin to pray that God's will be done. After a while I recite the Lord's Prayer over and over, while I work, while walking, whenever I can, because I don't know what to say to God anymore. I know what I want: I long for my sons to stop wrecking their young lives, and to be freed from the bitterness eating at their hearts. I long for my husband's depression to be overcome. I long for God's victory in our family life, for his kingdom to break into our lives.

And in this last longing, I begin to see a way forward. Up till now, I have been too concerned with finding a solution for myself, an end to my struggling. I have tried too hard to run a tight ship, been a slave too preoccupied with efficiency and perfection. I have been loveless, and lacked sufficient feeling for my husband's deep need.

Forgiveness—both asking for it and granting it—now gains an importance it never had in my life. We go into family therapy. We try to concentrate on finding the right priorities in our lives, and we try to seek for God in one another. At a retreat, we broaden our horizons by opening our eyes and ears to the burdens of others, and through this find new courage to share our own. I blurt out my despair, and a woman tells me simply, "Hold firm. And pray." She says it quietly, resolutely, with the sincerity that has known suffering, and it fills me with new hope.

And it begins to dawn on me just how powerful true prayer is. I had no glimpse of it back when life was normal. It was our helplessness that forced us to our knees. We are as empty now, as then, but we are certain God will help us. He alone has the answers we need—to our children's waywardness, my husband's depression, and the despair that attacks me. So we keep praying!

There are still battles, but if there weren't, how could there be victories? My husband and I pray that God will continue to lead us. We pray for the many who have worse needs than our own to carry. We pray for an earth assailed with unfathomable suffering.

Though Janine clearly has some very big problems in her family, there are few people who have not experienced similar heartache, at least in some measure. We have all been through times when God seemed very far away. Periods of spiritual drought, when it felt like the rain would never come. Periods of anguish or intense despair, such as when a beloved spouse or child dies.

Where is God?...Go to him when your need is desperate, when all other help is vain, and what do you find? A door slammed in your face, and a sound of bolting and double bolting on the inside. After that, silence. You may as well turn away…There are no lights in the windows. It might be an empty house. Was it ever inhabited? It seemed so once. What can this mean? Why is he so present in our time of prosperity and so very absent in time of trouble?

C.S. Lewis

Even the most sincere, the most deeply founded in faith, go through hours of despair. At such times it is important to continue praying. Perhaps it will sound as if we are talking into an echo chamber. Or perhaps we will feel that our efforts are so insignificant, so weak, that our voice can never reach heaven. But prayer never depends on our feeling close to God; he is always close to us, and he does hear us.

Janine found relief in talking things out, in sharing her plight with others. Such openness may seem appalling, in the sense that it invites vulnerability. But it can lead to healing and new courage, even if not to a resolution of the problem. Janine also held on by trying to concentrate on the good parts of her life: at least she is with her husband, and her children have not run away.

Corinne, a mother of four teenagers, lives in Philadelphia. Her husband is incarcerated three hundred miles away, and she has lost three of her children to the streets. Recently she shared her troubles with me:

My boys can make much more money running drugs than taking a job, and anyway my youngest is too young to work. I know he is not just using drugs, he's addicted to them. He's been using marijuana for at least two years, and I'm sure he's on to stronger things than that. I've already

lost him to the streets. I have a great fear that he will die
as a result of violence. I've already begged the state to put
him in a residential rehab program so he can at least have a
chance. I pray for him all the time. I do try to create a sense
of family, I have always been strict with my children, who
they associate with, but it's just not enough, with all the
temptations of the street right outside our front door.

Corinne's situation is far more typical than we might pre-
sume, as drugs and other pervasive social ills continue to rip
families apart. What can we say to comfort such a woman?

> Sometimes
> I feel old
> useless
> and ugly
> I reach and nothing comes
> I speak and no one hears
> I sing and no heart is moved
> But then I pray
> And Lord
> You listen
> *Theresa Greenwood*

The distress of these mothers, the bitter anguish that comes
from their God-given love for their children, and many
times also from self-accusation, cannot simply be relieved
with well-meant words of comfort. Perseverance in prayer
for their sons and daughters is indeed their only weapon.
But they need to be helped to believe that in each person's
deepest hidden center there is a spark from God, and that,
even if a person is seemingly lost to grace, ultimately God
is in control.

There is no one who is so weak or sinful that God will not hear him. As the nineteenth-century evangelist Charles Finney put it:

> The very fact that prayer is so great a privilege to sinners, makes it most honorable to God to hear prayer...He who regards alike the flight of an archangel and the fall of a sparrow—before whose eyes no event is too minute for his attention, no insect too small for his notice—his infinite glory is manifest in this very fact, that nothing is too lofty or too low for his regard. None are too insignificant for his sympathy—none too mean to share his kindness.

Teresa was nineteen when she was imprisoned and sentenced to death in 1982, and Miriam, my neighbor, has been corresponding with her almost ever since. Miriam says that if there is anything Teresa knows well, it is despair, which she has struggled with even since her sentence was commuted to life imprisonment. In August 1989 Teresa wrote:

> The parole board wants me to do eight more years before I come up for parole again. That will be in January 1997. I thought I would feel a bit more at ease after I did seven years, but now things seem to be even worse. I feel like I am starting this time over again but in a harder prison.

How long is seven years? Write a letter to Teresa once a week for seven years, and you'll have some idea. And how long are eight more after that? Teresa writes:

> I've gotten to the point where I don't care about anything anymore, and I just want to give up. I don't even dream anymore of what I'll do when I get home, because I feel like I'll never leave here. This place makes me give up on any kind of good future that I maybe could have had.

I have gotten so angry and bitter with the people here that I have backslid very far. I see myself turning cold, and I don't like it. I do believe in God, and know that's who I need in my life, but it seems so much harder to turn my life over to him this time. Please keep praying for me.

In 1995 Teresa's parole was denied for another three years. Then in May 1998 came another blow:

I found out this weekend that the parole board has asked for eight *more* years. I am okay, but I am hurt, and my Dad was really sad because he could not help me get out. But I am still trusting in God to do a miracle for me.

After getting this news, Miriam asked Teresa what she felt like when God answered her prayers with a no. Teresa's answer came in the form of this poem:

I don't pretend to know the answer;
    I can't seem to understand.
If God can answer all my prayers,
    where is he when I need a hand?
When I cried out for freedom
    from behind my prison walls,
He hid himself in silence
    and ignored my anguished calls...
It's not as if my trust has crumbled;
    I won't take it as my fate;
I still have faith that he will let me
    through the shining gate.
So in the meantime, when I'm down,
    and dreary days grow long,
I'll do just like that prisoner, Paul:
    stand patient, firm and strong.

Sophie Scholl was a twenty-one-year-old university student who was active in the "White Rose," an underground movement that resisted Hitler's Third Reich. During her brief imprisonment in Munich in February 1943 (she was executed only a few days after her arrest) she wrote to her boyfriend, Fritz, on the Russian front:

> The only remedy for a barren heart is prayer, however poor and inadequate...We must pray, and pray for each other, and if you were here, I'd fold hands with you, because we're poor, weak, sinful children. Oh, Fritz, if I can't write anything else just now, it's only because there's a terrible absurdity about a drowning man who, instead of calling for help, launches into a scientific, philosophical, or theological dissertation while the sinister tentacles of the creatures on the seabed are encircling his arms and legs, and the waves are breaking over him. It's only because I'm filled with fear, that and nothing else, and feel an undivided yearning for him who can relieve me of it.
>
> I'm still so remote from God that I don't even sense his presence when I pray. Sometimes when I utter God's name, in fact, I feel like sinking into a void. It isn't a frightening or dizzying sensation, it's nothing at all—and that's far more terrible. But prayer is the only remedy for it, and however many devils scurry around inside me, I shall cling to the rope God has thrown me, even if my numb hands can no longer feel it.

The Bible is full of stories of men and women who, like Sophie, felt abandoned but clung to God anyway. Psalm 130, one of my favorites, begins: "Out of the depths I cry to thee, O Lord! Hear my voice, be attentive to my supplications." If King David, and even the prophets of Israel, felt themselves to be in such depths of despair, why should we be spared? Yet we can also take comfort in the words at the end of the same psalm: "Hope in the Lord, for with him there is steadfast love and plenteous redemption."

Abraham called the place where God tested his faith by requiring the sacrifice of his only son, "God sees." God sees and knows everything. We humans see only what is visible, whereas God looks at the heart. And therefore we must trust that he knows what is behind every appearance. There is nothing that does not open to his sight. Sometimes a person does something we do not understand, or says something stupid or clumsy, but his intention was quite different—God knows what was in the heart; he hears what remains unspoken.

It may seem frightening to be penetrated by the clear light of God's gaze. But we ought never to forget that even in judgment God sees us with eyes of love. When God sees his children, he affirms them and encourages them. His love is redemptive; it is the power that enables us to become our true selves. He sees the evil in a person so clearly and sharply, it is as if he had no love for him; at the same time he hopes so strongly for that person, it is as if he saw no evil in him. Even his harshest words of condemnation are spoken with the most tender love. That is why we can do nothing better than to place ourselves willingly under his light and say, "God, see me as I am, and see me for what I long to be."

Augustine says that when a carpenter walks through the woods, he does not see the trees as they stand there in the forest, but as the beams of the house they will be made into. So God has joy in us, not as we are now but what we can be. As Archbishop Desmond Tutu puts it: "God does not look at the caterpillar we are now but at the dazzling butterfly we have it in us to become." We must ask for eyes to see each other with the same hope and love.

When Laura married Basil, their wedding brought tremendous joy to all of us who knew them. Yet soon after they had a child, Basil left her, and Laura was left to raise her son without a father. Laura loves her husband and remains faithful to him. There seems little chance of these two ever coming together again, but Laura believes God sees her need, and who can debate that? Prayer opens doors.

> Even though my husband is unfaithful, I often feel very close to him through prayer. Strange as it may seem, I even feel what a gift it is to be able to carry him inwardly in this way, and place our marriage in God's hands.
>
> I don't know what will happen at all, but if he returns I will look back on this time as foundational – a gift to learn that pain is real, to live in prayer, and to experience that God comes close to us when we are in pain.
>
> I often remember what someone once said to me about being close to God in suffering. It's a whole dimension of a full life to have awful outward conditions and totally, in spite of it, to experience a deeper fulfillment than ever.
>
> For me, prayer is like the fourth dimension or the sixth sense, and life is only half there without it. Prayer is like a whole, real, other side of life that gives all relationships meaning, because with prayer you can suffer with other people's suffering, even if you can't do anything about it.

Generations of children have loved the story of Jonah, who was sent by God to call the people of Nineveh to repentance, but disobeyed and boarded a ship in a cowardly and foolish effort to escape his notice. A mighty storm came, and the ship was almost lost. But as the desperate crew threw the cargo overboard and prayed to their gods, Jonah lay fast asleep. He was wakened by the captain, and the sailors drew lots to see whose fault it was that such a calamity had come upon them. The lot fell to Jonah. He confessed that he was running away from God and had them throw him overboard. Immediately the sea ceased its raging, but Jonah was swallowed by a whale. Three days later he was thrown up on dry land. This time, obedient to God, he struck out for Nineveh.

While in the belly of the whale, Jonah prayed:

In my distress I called to the Lord, and he answered me. From the depths of the grave I called for help, and you listened to my cry. You hurled me into the deep, into the very heart of the seas, and the currents swirled about me; all your waves and breakers swept over me. I said, "I have been banished from your sight; yet I will look again toward your holy temple." The engulfing waters threatened me, the deep surrounded me; seaweed was wrapped around my head. To the roots of the mountains I sank down; the earth beneath barred me in forever. But you brought my life up from the pit, O Lord my God. When my life was ebbing away, I remembered you, Lord, and my prayer rose to you, to your holy temple. Those who cling to worthless idols forfeit the grace that could be theirs. But I, with a song of thanksgiving, will sacrifice to you. What I have vowed I will make good. For my deliverance comes from God alone.

It would seem that Jonah was not the strongest of characters, yet God chose to use him and show us how he tries to draw us to himself in so many ways: through sharpness, through compassion, through mercy. He deals with us much as a loving parent would deal with wayward children.

My father Heinrich, a pastor for many decades, counseled many distressed souls over the years he served our church. At the same time, he himself suffered much, both physically and inwardly, but he was never downcast about it. Rather, he said he believed we do good only insofar as we are willing to go the way of Jesus, "from the manger to the cross." He even spoke of "embracing" the cross. For him this meant accepting suffering in whatever form it came, and accepting it gladly. In a letter he once wrote:

> The fact that we seek God at all in times of misfortune shows us that our deepest being hungers and thirsts for him. We should bring our fears to God; we should bring him our sickness and anguish. But that is not enough. We must give him our innermost being, our heart and soul. When we humble ourselves before him in this way, and give ourselves completely over to him – when we no longer resist giving him our whole person, our whole personality – then he can help us.

Papa always encouraged people to look beyond their personal struggles or hardships and to seek a greater vision – to consider God's desire to redeem the whole world of its need and despair. God expressed this longing through the prophet Isaiah:

> Come, all you who are thirsty,
>   come to the waters;
> and you who have no money,
>   come, buy and eat!
> Come, buy wine and milk
>   without money and without cost.

Why spend money on what is not bread,
and your labor on what does not satisfy?
Listen, listen to me, and eat what is good,
and you will delight in the richest of fare.

Isa. 55:1–2

9.

attitude

Everything in life is affected by our attitude, whether we are getting a job done, playing a game, or singing in a choir. The same is true for prayer.

We all know the story of the children of Israel, who turned to God when they needed him, but ignored him when things were going well. How do we measure up? Poet Kahlil Gibran admonishes: "You pray in your distress and in your need; would that you might also pray in the fullness of your joy and in your days of abundance."

Abraham Lincoln, conscious of the same spiritual laziness in the United States of his day, proclaimed "a national day of fasting, humiliation, and prayer" in 1863. His words at the time are even truer today than when they were first spoken—a telling comment on our present condition.

> We have forgotten God...Intoxicated with unbroken success, we have become too self-sufficient to feel the necessity of redeeming and preserving grace—too proud to pray to the God who made us! It behooves us, then, to humble ourselves before the offended Power, to confess our national sins, and to pray for clemency and forgiveness.

Too many of us forget God when we are healthy and happy, when we are doing well. But God needs people who carry the depth of their belief out into the world every day, people who not only appeal to him in times of distress, but who pay him homage because they love him.

In the busyness of our lives, we often neglect the things of the spirit, and our relationship with God becomes luke-warm. Rick, a friend who works as a sales manager, tells me:

In my life, being busy is a big obstacle to prayer. There is seemingly so much to do. Society moves at a rapid rate, and stress is more common than the common cold. I find myself caught up in busyness, trying to tackle my to-do list, but missing God. If I am honest, the big to-do list is self-inflicted, and the stress my own fault. The reality of the situation is that letting go of my busyness and turning to God is the only way to have a real life.

There are many things that stand in the way of our relating to God: inner laziness, hypocrisy, pride, lack of faith, self-centeredness. All of these are impediments to a meaning-ful relationship with God, and therefore require us to take a stand against them. It is a question of deciding what our attitude will be, and then working to stick to that decision.

Insofar as the self pushes for its own way, it hinders the working of God. In each of us there is an unfathomable mass of ideas and emotions that are neither concentrated on God nor at one with his will—this is simply a fact of human nature. And because of it, our prayers will always be burdened by our personal failings and by the weight of self. That is why the Lord's Prayer says: "Forgive us our sins; deliver us from evil."

Eberhard Arnold

Many people have experienced that a burdened conscience blocks their communication with God. For example, a woman wrote to me about a Gulf War veteran who told her that he had done terrible things during the war, and that since then he has been unable to pray. He was desperate: "I can't talk to God anymore. Pray for me, that I can learn to pray again."

Often a sense of guilt does indeed block our way to God. Yet if we are truly repentant, we will find someone we trust to whom we can speak out our sins and shortcomings. It is true that forgiveness comes from God alone, but an open and honest confession has a mysterious power; through it complete freeing can be given, the soul healed, and the relationship with God restored. As the apostle James advises, "Confess your sins to one another, and pray for one another, that you may be healed." In *The Cost of Discipleship*, Dietrich Bonhoeffer writes:

> No one should be surprised at the difficulty of faith, if there is some part of his life where he is consciously resisting or disobeying the commandments of God. Is there some part of your life that you are refusing to surrender at his behest, some sinful passion, maybe, or some animosity, some hope, perhaps your ambition or your reason? If so, you must not be surprised that you have not received the Holy Spirit, that prayer is difficult, or that your request for faith remains unanswered.

Insincerity is a hindrance in all our relationships. Ignatius writes to the Ephesians: "It is better to be silent and *be*, than to talk and not be." Honesty demands that our words be backed up by our actions.

Jesus, too, speaks sharply against hypocrisy: "Woe to you, scribes and Pharisees, hypocrites! For you are like whitewashed tombs, which on the outside look beautiful, but inside they are full of the bones of the dead and of all

kinds of filth" (Matt. 23:27). We are also instructed to lock
ourselves in our rooms and pray in secret so that God, who
sees in secret, will reward us. I have always felt that the point
was not so much privacy as humility.

In order to warn us against self-righteousness, Jesus tells
a parable about two men who went to the Temple to pray.
One was a Pharisee, a member of a Jewish sect known for
its strict adherence to the letter of the Law. The other was a
tax collector. The first prayed: "I thank thee, O God, that I
am not like other people, extortioners, unjust, adulterers, or
even like this tax collector. I fast twice a week, I give tithes
of all that I get." The tax collector, however, stood at a dis-
tance, and without even lifting his eyes to heaven, beat his
breast and pleaded: "O God, have mercy on me, a sinner."
Jesus says that it was the tax collector who was acquitted of
his sins, "for everyone who exalts himself will be humbled,
but he who humbles himself will be exalted."

Some time ago I had the privilege of meeting Archbishop
Desmond Tutu of South Africa. During our conversation,
he told me that his favorite biblical text is in Romans 5,
where it says that "Christ died for us while we were still
sinners," because it shows we have been loved long before
we ever do anything to deserve being loved. He noted that
people who come out of a culture of success and achieve-
ment find it difficult to accept the unmerited grace of God.
It is really the same with prayer: we are given the grace to
have a relationship with God independent of our achieve-
ments or pride of self.

Related to pride is egotism, which often leads us into self-
centered prayer. That is the heart of the "prosperity gos-

pel," where people pray unabashedly for wealth, success in their careers, and other mundane things. Such trivial prayer belittles God.

The Lord's Prayer begins with God, and not with ourselves or our own needs. To use the words of St. Francis: "Let us be ashamed to be caught up in worthless imaginings, for at the time of prayer, we speak to the great King." We have been told to ask so that we might receive, and been promised that anyone who seeks will find, and those who knock will find the door opened to them. But in all our prayers we should bring glory to God, not to ourselves.

Often we are caught up in our important activities and no longer see the working of God around us. The story of Balaam in the Old Testament shows us how blind we can be. This prophet was so full of his own ideas and intentions that God literally made fun of him. It was the time of Israel's wandering in the desert, and the king of Moab was worried about this great tribe encamped near him. He called on Balaam, a Gentile prophet, to curse the Israelites. Balaam asked God for permission, and God told him he should not do it. But Balaam, against God's word, set off on his donkey toward the Israelite camp the next morning.

He had not gone far before God decided to intervene. An angel stood in the road with sword drawn. The donkey saw the angel, but Balaam did not: he had lost touch with God's will, being so full of his own. The donkey had the good sense to step aside, which earned him a beating from Balaam. Three times the angel stood in the way. Balaam got increasingly annoyed at his donkey, who kept trying to detour around the angel. The third time the angel chose a narrow spot on the road where the donkey couldn't turn either way. The donkey sat down. Balaam started thrashing the donkey with a stick, still blind to the messenger of God standing right in front of him.

Then God "opened the donkey's mouth." And the donkey didn't just beg for mercy. He lectured the prophet: "Why are you beating me? What did I ever do to you? Am I not your obedient donkey that you've ridden all your life?" Balaam was stopped short. He felt stupid—and chastened. And suddenly he could see the angel.

Like stupidity or spiritual blindness, unforgiveness can also block the way to God. Jesus said our sins would be forgiven to the extent that we forgive others, yet how few of us take this seriously! I am sure many prayers are not heard because the person praying is holding a grudge. Writer Anna Mow says:

> If my heart is hard toward anyone, it is closed also toward God. God forgives. That is his nature. He is real love. So my forgiving relationship with others is the determining factor in my reception of the forgiveness of God. This is the bridge over which every Christian must pass. The secret of power in prayer lies right here.

Another serious obstacle to the working of God in our lives is unbelief—or at least the shallowness that causes our faith to waver with every emotion. The following story from the gospels wonderfully emphasizes the importance of a deeply-grounded faith:

> When they came to the crowd, a man approached Jesus and knelt before him. "Lord, have mercy on my son," he said. "He has seizures and is suffering greatly. He often falls into the fire or into the water. I brought him to your disciples, but they could not heal him."

"O unbelieving and perverse generation," Jesus replied, "how long shall I stay with you? How long shall I put up with you? Bring the boy here to me." Jesus rebuked the demon, and it came out of the boy, and he was healed from that moment.

Then the disciples came to Jesus in private and asked, "Why couldn't we drive it out?" He replied, "Because you have so little faith. I tell you the truth, if you have faith as small as a mustard seed, you can say to this mountain, 'Move from here to there,' and it will move. Nothing will be impossible for you, but this kind never comes out except by prayer and fasting."

Matt. 17:14–21

The point of this story is not so much the fasting, nor even perhaps the healing, but faith. We are weak people, weak in our faith and in our devotion to God. But how big is a mustard seed? Very small, yet it contains everything it needs to grow. We, too, should have everything within ourselves: the deep faith that Jesus speaks of, a childlike trust in God, and the courage to face difficulties. Most important, we must have love. As Paul tells us in his First Letter to the Corinthians, without love even faith is not enough.

I have often been asked if it is really possible that an almighty Being would allow one of us, small and weak as we are, to contact him directly. Is it truly possible that he is influenced in some way by our prayers? God is so infinitely great, and we so infinitely small, so unworthy of his attention, that this seems unimaginable. On the other hand, when we turn to God, we do so precisely because of our weakness. In praying, we are asking God to do something we cannot do, to help us because we cannot help ourselves, to change something because we cannot change it.

Dick, a close friend, writes:

If God is not there, then we are alone in dealing with our feelings, and it is an impersonal, mechanistic universe; in times of deepest need we will feel truly lost. None of us completely understands himself. If I believe I am alone, then I try to observe myself, heal myself, manage myself, guide myself, and in the process I split myself into observer and observed, manager and managed, physician and patient, and so forth. This inner division is intolerable for the soul.

God is love. He loves the poor and humble especially. It is his will to reveal himself to the meek, the poor in spirit. And he has promised his living water, his spirit, to anyone who asks for it. Only in this flowing river of God's power can our faith be living. Out of it, our faith dies like a fish on dry land.

Therefore we must really believe, when we pray, that God hears us. And we must believe that our prayers, poor as they may seem, can change even the history of the world. That is, we must have faith that through our pleading the breaking in of God's kingdom – the promised reign of justice, peace, and love – will take place.

There is no barrier, no wall or mountain, too high for the prayer of faith. God is above everything, and his spirit is stronger than all other spirits. When a person's faith, life, and deeds are in the spirit of Jesus, his prayers will be answered. Everything we do must have one goal: that God's kingdom comes on earth and that his will takes place on earth. He can then show us that he is greater than our hearts can grasp, and greater things will happen than we would dare to put into words. His answer will surpass our boldest imaginings.

When author Dale Aukerman, a long-time friend, was diagnosed with cancer, he was told there was no hope for a cure and was given only a few months to live. In his own life he has experienced the paradox of strength being given in our frailty and weakness. Two years later he wrote:

> God has worked the gracious miracle of extending my life. A great many have been praying for me. We give praise to God, who has heard the prayers and given a gracious measure of healing…There remains a problematic aspect. Many have prayed fervently that I be completely healed of the cancer. Some have told me they felt an assurance that such healing would be given. I'm doing remarkably well, but the tumor in the left lung, though shrunken, is still one and one-half inches across. Though the grave threat continues, what stands out for us is answered prayer and prolonged life. I struggle with this issue of full healing, not mainly on my own account, but because healing prayed for but not given looms as a central puzzle for Christians.
>
> A friend expressed to me one type of approach. She promised me: if I would have one hundred percent faith that God was going to heal me, that would most certainly come about. In this sort of view, complete healing has not been given me because of a lack of faith.

But if Dale or anyone had complete certainty that God will heal us or perform any other miracle we ask of him, then we would be totally filled with our own hopes and not open to God's will for us. It is another paradox: on the one hand we must have complete faith in what God can do for us, but on the other we must remain open for his will in our lives. And who are we to say that a suffering person lacks sufficient faith?

The Book of Job tells the story of a man who struggles to accept suffering. God and Satan are in conflict concerning human faith. Satan ridicules the faith of the righteous Job, saying he would only remain true in good times. God decides to prove Satan wrong by allowing him to put Job to the test. As readers, we understand the cosmic significance of what is happening, but Job does not. His riches are taken away, his children die, and he is afflicted with "loathsome sores and boils from the sole of his foot to the crown of his head." Job must respond without understanding, in simple trust.

Job is not a silent martyr. He cries out with all his mind and strength for meaning, and rebels against the senselessness of his situation. But in his heart, he hangs on to his faith and refuses to curse God.

The story has a larger significance. Each human being must decide for or against belief—belief in God despite all the absurdity of human suffering. And the overarching conflict between good and evil is decided by the choices we make. The story ends with God giving Job back doubly what was taken away. It is a picture of the kingdom of God, when all suffering will be rewarded, all contradictions resolved, and we will finally understand. The book leaves many questions unanswered, but it reaffirms the sense that our struggles and suffering are not unnoticed by God—and certainly not meaningless.

Even if we have found some measure of faith, there will still be spiritually dry times. Then we have to persist in prayer, knowing that every believer goes through times of darkness and times of light in his or her prayer life.

One evening, when Jesus wanted to spend some time alone in prayer, he sent his disciples out on the lake. Later he appeared, walking across the water toward them. The disciples were fearful at first, thinking it a ghost, but Jesus reassured them, and invited Peter to walk to him on the water. Peter began, but soon became afraid and began to sink. Jesus immediately reached out his hand, caught him, and chided him for his lack of faith.

Even the strongest person goes through moments when he or she loses faith. Then one has to "walk on the water." And Jesus said that faith even as small as a mustard seed is sufficient. He understands our weakness. He was once one of us.

So much depends on how we approach God. Are we trusting, expectant, childlike? The so-called "mentally retarded" are wonderfully graced with freedom from many, if not all, of the obstacles I have mentioned in this chapter. They are free from the bondage of the intellect, and in their childlikeness and purity of heart they do not know hypocrisy, envy, or pride. Their faith stands firm and unshakable in the face of seeming impossibilities.

Lois Ann, a neighbor whose daughter Louisa had Down Syndrome, remembers how, when her congregation was working through a crisis, Louisa obtained a complete list of all members. Sitting by the window with it, she slowly read each person's name aloud, glancing up to the sky after each one. It took her several days.

At a church I visited this past summer there was concern for an expectant mother; it appeared that the baby she was carrying was developing abnormally. The parents shared their fears with the pastor and asked for intercession, and at the next service, prayers were said for the baby and mother.

At an appointment the following week, to everyone's utter amazement, the baby was found to be perfect in every way. The doctors were astonished. Later the mother wrote:

It was a real answer to our prayers. But what meant the most to me was that when we spoke about it at church, I noticed how Lisa—a young woman with Down Syndrome—was blowing her nose and wiping her eyes, and I realized how much she was carrying our need. Honestly, I don't know if God always hears my prayers—there is so much in me each day that stands in his way—but I know for sure that he hears Lisa's. I've had to think that I may never know how much we owe to the prayers of someone like her.

10.

reverence

Conditions were primitive and rough in the back-woods of Paraguay, where I grew up in the 1940s, and the harshness of daily life had an effect not only on many adults, but also on us children, who reacted to their callousness with disrespect and mockery. Nothing was sacred, despite the efforts some parents made to instill respect in their children, and we were often cruelly insensitive to the peculiarities and afflictions of other people.

Anybody can be mean, but in the culture of today, mean-spiritedness has become a way of life. Violence, promiscuity, arrogance, snideness, and indifference mark modern culture. At the bottom of it all is a cynicism that not only corrodes individual relationships; it destroys our relationship with God. If one were to describe our time with one word, that word would have to be irreverence.

What, then, is reverence?

It is the spiritual side of respect. It is nothing pious, soft, or sweet. Reverence is wonder at what God has created; it is man's standing in awe of what God has made. He is the creator of life in all its rich and varied forms—exquisite flowers and magnificent trees, tiny insects and colorful birds, creatures on the land and in the sea.

There is no doubt that life has an immensely high value, both human life and the life of animals and plants; yes, even the life of stars and stones. I am convinced that not only animals have an emotional life-feeling; I am convinced that plants, too, have a life-feeling. It is unthinkable that the beauty of plants and their swaying in the wind, the moving upward and downward of the sap in their stems could exist without any life-feeling. And I believe more: I believe that astronomical organisms, like the stars and the earth, have a life-feeling. In a fiery star like our sun with its flaming protuberances and its deepening solar spots there is no doubt a living soul; one could even speak of a breathing process.

Eberhard Arnold

Reverence is our natural, unspoiled response to the marvels of God's creation. We experience it when we witness the birth of a baby, the power of a storm and the glory of a rainbow, and often when we are sitting at the bedside of a person who is dying. Reverence is the movement of our hearts that comes to us through a piece of music or writing, through a work of art in painting or sculpture, when these are born from the creative spirit God gives to his children. It can be spoken, or it can simply be felt.

Without reverence, God is pushed aside, and our lower nature comes to the fore, our bitter, cynical self-will. Then we forget that all life is sacred. Then we are not far from accepting abortion and capital punishment, euthanasia and assisted suicide as acceptable ways to deal with seemingly unbearable or insoluble problems.

I believe every person begins life with an inborn sense of reverence. But this must be nurtured and protected. It can grow, or it can be crushed. I don't believe it can ever be completely lost in anyone, although it certainly may be dulled. It may take years to win it back again if a person has lived with an attitude of irreverence for a long time; many people have told me this. Cynicism, once established, is hard to eradicate, for by its very definition it mocks the essence of what is true and good in life – the spark of God in each person, the eternal that is in every soul.

Reverence as a spiritual concept may be foreign to some people, and yet it is a crucial dimension to all our relationships, including our relationship to God. Without it one cannot pray.

My wife received the following letter from Anneta, a nurse we know who volunteered for several months at a hospital in rural Haiti. Anneta's thoughts shed light on the significance of reverence – and on the unredeemed rawness of life where it has been snuffed out.

> After delivering twelve babies into this world as of today, I ponder the significance of these births to my life, the life of the children, and to God.
>
> *Me:* God has placed me here now and is allowing me to participate in his creation. So often during labor and delivery, fear twists my stomach instead of wonder and joy. So many things can and often do go wrong. Afterwards I mostly just feel relief that it went okay, or heaviness when it didn't. My shallowness of faith prevents me from rejoicing in the majesty of God's creation and his plan for each soul. My helplessness is often so evident. I believe I am here now for God to show me that I am nothing, how in the past year I have placed myself in the way of God's working and selfishly took things into my own hands. Lord, I pray that Haiti teaches me complete surrender of *all* life to you. Forgive my arrogance and prepare me for your use.

The babies: I often wonder what life holds for you, *petit*—the tough, sad faces of your mothers, the blatant absence of your fathers, the grueling work, and the terrible fear. Yet each life is created by God for a purpose.

And God: The ones you send for a few minutes or hours or days—my inmost depth wonders at the meaning of these small lives—they are like spoken words of yours, and those stillborn just your thoughts. I think of my own culture and of the anguish of my friend Paula in America over her still-born baby, and her tears and weeping months later at the grave. And here in Haiti the dry eyes and quietness, the immediate resumption of life when a baby dies. After nine months—the lack of attachment. Do they lose so many that they can't afford to grieve? I feel a small corner of your power and mystery, yet I am not sufficiently in tune with you to understand it all. My soul marvels in reverence for you and I pray for depth in you.

The following month Anneta wrote again:

I went over to maternity, where another nurse and I delivered a little baby girl who was missing her skull bones. She only had a face; the rest of her head was missing. Her brain was exposed, open. We have had her mother in the ward for a long time and had done an ultrasound, so we were expecting the baby to have problems, but it was still a very shaking experience. She never seemed to breathe, but her little heart beat for twenty minutes. Hundreds of people crowded in to look at the "creature" or "frog" as they called her. I chased them out, but most of them came right back in, and my heart was aching too much to enforce it...

I picked up the little one, holding her disfigured premature body until the heart stopped, then laid her down, covering her head with a latex glove to protect her from mockery...I was overwhelmed and couldn't stop crying, although it was not out of grief that I cried—more out of a strange, painful joy. I felt as if I had been drawn closer to heaven.

Some days are extremely difficult, and I rely on prayer hourly to get me through. I am so privileged to be here with these people and to be allowed to experience pain, birth, and death with them. One night last week I delivered a little boy from a mother with polyhydramnios. He was very premature, and his abdomen was swollen and hard. I tried resuscitating him, but it soon became clear that this child would not live long.

His heart beat very slowly, and I wrapped him in blankets and took him over to his mother. She looked at me with big, tear-filled eyes and nodded quietly. A crowd of onlookers surrounded us, and I asked if any of them wanted to hold the little one. All smiled and politely declined, so I held him tight. The families here will never touch or take the body of a stillborn child, or even of a deformed newborn, unless they think it will live. Of course, I can never judge how someone else deals with life and death; these people have taught me so much. Perhaps it is just their way of coping.

As I stand there in the stench of a pool of amniotic fluid and blood, a single dim light bulb barely holding back the edges of night, lizards and flies around our feet, the soul of that little baby reaches out to mine, melting the past, present, future of worries and the weary struggle of life into undiluted pureness of awe. I grasp him close as his heartbeat slows and fades away. My eyes are filled with tears, my heart both torn and stretched.

I put the little one down and go to find a cardboard box from the pharmacy—one just the right size so that no part of his body is bent, which is important to the family. Andres, the janitor, will take him away tomorrow.

Young children with their natural guilelessness can teach us much about reverence. They are genuine and sincere, without ulterior motives. With them, there is no danger of practicing their piety in front of other people. And children sing—unselfconsciously and happily, thus expressing their connectedness to God more beautifully than the most eloquent prayer. Children are generously forgiving, and they abandon themselves completely in their enjoyment of life. In short, children are reverent.

But this reverence, this childlike spirit, must be protected. We should never force children to say prayers (let alone memorize long ones), for then their innate longing to speak to God may be harmed. More important than regular prayers is preserving in our children their natural longing for what is of God. And in doing this, we also preserve our own reverence. I have been told by several articulate, highly educated people that when it comes to prayer, they use the simplest words and relate to God just as a child would.

My grandfather, Eberhard Arnold, was a theologian. I never knew him, but I have been told that he was not an overtly religious person. Things of the spirit were simply natural to him, and after a few minutes in his presence you knew that all that mattered in his life was Christ. Even so, he did not teach his children much from the Bible; he must have had too much of it himself as a child. Papa told me that when he was sixteen years old, he discovered the Lord's Prayer on his own and was amazed that such a prayer existed; his father had never mentioned it to him. My grandfather led his children to faith through his actions.

My wife and I have over forty grandchildren, and we notice again and again how close young children are to God. They

will speak trustingly of their guardian angels, and they love
to sing the lullaby from Humperdinck's *Hansel and Gretel:*

> When at night I go to sleep
> Fourteen angels watch do keep:
> Two my head are guarding,
> Two my feet are guiding,
> Two are on my right hand,
> Two are on my left hand,
> Two who warmly cover,
> Two who o'er me hover,
> Two to whom 'tis given
> To guide my steps to heaven.

True children—that is, those who are still childlike—have
no doubt that this is true. And in these times we grown-ups,
too, are in need of protection, day and night, by the unseen
powers from heaven.

Recently a child said to me, "I'm frightened when I hear
about wars and bombs, and people getting killed. It gives me
nightmares!" How far should we go in exposing our children
to the need of the world? It is a difficult question. Certainly
we cannot bring them up in protective isolation, yet on the
other hand, we do not want to burden them unnecessarily
with thoughts and images of violence and hunger, disease
and death. Perhaps the balance is in making our children
aware of these things but at the same time helping them to
remember that God's angels are always watching over them.
What is happening in the world is certainly terrible, but we
must believe that, ultimately, God will create a new heaven
and a new earth. This is promised us in the Book of Revelation: "He will wipe away every tear from our eyes, death
will be no more; sadness and crying and pain will pass away."

Jesus taught us reverence for children. He said, "Let the little children come to me, and do not hinder them, for the kingdom of God belongs to them." And, "Assuredly I say to you, whoever does not receive the kingdom of God as a little child will not enter it." And then, "See that you do not look down on one of these little ones. For I tell you that their angels in heaven always see the face of my father."

If you are around children very much, you will soon see how trusting they are, and how dependent on us. When you sit by a child at bedtime, you can feel how necessary it is that the child find an inner contact with God. You can tell him that high above the stars there is someone who is good, someone who knows and loves him. He may say, "I know who you mean; the angels are up there above the stars."

"Yes, but above the angels is someone still greater. It is God."

Then the child may feel something of this great being, the Creator who is above all things and yet is always close to us. We can tell the child, "In your heart, you can feel this good and great God; you can speak to him, and obey him."

This is important, for obedience comes through listening. And when we learn to listen to the inner voice of the living God, then we can learn to obey him. In such a way we can help our children to realize that the voice of their conscience is actually the voice of God at work in them. There is such a voice in the depth of every heart. Even the young child knows when he has done something wrong, and this works in his heart and makes him restless and unhappy until he is stirred to put it right. And so the child can be led to an understanding of the power of good over evil and to a living faith in God.

Rudi, a lifelong friend, was a seven-year-old orphan when my grandparents took him into their family in the early 1920s. When he arrived, he was frightened and cried bitterly at the prospect of yet another home. He remembers:

> My fears about a new orphanage were soon gone, for this was a real home. Eberhard took me on his lap and told me that he would be my father and Emmy my mother (it was like that until they died). Still, I longed to have my real parents, and I wept often.
>
> My new parents comforted me and told me about God. From that time on, peace slowly came into my heart and I felt the need to pray every evening. My prayer was not just for myself, but also to thank God for all the good things we had, even though we were extremely poor: for my bed, for my shoes, or for the extra piece of bread we had that day.

In my previous book *Seeking Peace* I included an anecdote from Magdalena, a woman I have known since childhood, about the death of her little brother, and the death of her mother several years later. She has since told me the following:

> When I was fourteen years old, my mother became very sick. Most of her life she had suffered from asthma, and so her heart was weakened. We children were told that Mama needed a big operation, and because of her heart condition she might not live through it. This came as a terrible shock to us. Our mother, with her joy and her tenderness, was really the heart of the family.
>
> Like never before, I went down on my knees and pleaded to God for our mother's life. I promised to serve God for the rest of my days and to give up all my wickedness if only God would preserve her life.

Mama lived through the surgery, and her life was spared, even though she never regained her full strength. She lived a few more years before she died during an asthma attack.

I truly believe that my prayer for Mama was answered. At that time I found a relationship with God that has lasted until now. Although I was still very young, I knew from then on that I could always turn to him, but I also knew I had promised to serve him and must do my part.

We should never underestimate the power of children's prayers. Adults tend to be divided, untruthful, and insincere; many of us live double lives. Yet children are single-hearted. Because they are close to God, their prayers, simple as they are, can turn hearts of stone into hearts of flesh.

11.

letting go

In my work as a pastor and counselor, I realize more and more the importance of helping others to "let go," and to see that, in the end, all our human striving comes to nothing. Too often people exert themselves in trying to solve a problem their way, and realize later that their preoccupation does nothing but worsen the situation. In such cases it is better to leave it in God's hands and let him take care of it.

There are times when one's prayer life becomes a battlefield, and prayer becomes a fight rather than a meditation. At such times prayer is no quick and easy way out of a troubling situation, but a harrowing process of working things through until the heart is cleansed. Anyone who has had to face intense personal distress will know just what I mean. Jeanne, a member of my church, relates what she experienced while expecting her second child:

It was shortly before Oliver was born, and already for a long time I had known that not everything was as it should be. But even on the worst days, I never thought we would lose our baby. When it became clear that the little life I was carrying had only a slim chance of making it, it was like my worst nightmare come true.

I knelt down, numb, and prayed, "Thy will be done." But then it hit me: "You hypocrite! You don't mean a word of it!" And I realized I didn't. I did not want God's will at all. I wanted my will. I wanted my baby. And if God meant to take him, then I wasn't going to have any part of it. Every fiber in my body rebelled against surrendering my child into his hands.

That was the end of my prayers for that night, but it was only the beginning of the struggle. I knew I had to get to the point where I could pray honestly, "Thy will be done," and truly mean it. Otherwise I would have no peace.

For many days all I could do was ask for "the will to want thy will." Sometimes it was very hard to pray. Medically, so many things were going wrong that my stomach was tied in knots and my heart filled with anxiety. God knows—perhaps those were days when my struggling and heartache and emptiness became prayer. In any case it was obvious that not even the most skilled doctors could change a thing. I didn't really have a choice. I had to let go of everything—all my longings as a mother for my child. It had to be all or nothing. Either I trusted God, or I didn't. Wasn't it far better to let go, and let God take over, than continue in this state of panic?

Bit by bit, my longing was answered. Gradually I felt peace, even joy, in letting go: "Here, God, my child is all yours." I had stopped fighting, and it was a tremendous relief. It still hurt, but the tension was gone; my prayers were like sobs in mother's arms.

Perhaps the greatest gift was Oliver's birth itself. I had had tremendous fear of it: how could I ever cope with having my baby die in my arms? But when the baby came, all my anxiety was lifted. It was simply gone. Oliver's birth, his short life span of two hours, and his dying were all experiences of the deepest peace.

There is still the pain of having lost this child almost before I was able to take him in. I still don't know "why," and sometimes I am still tempted by "what ifs." But my struggle to honestly submit to God's will, and the peace he then gave me, reassure me to this day.

There is a blessing and tremendous peace that comes, often unexpectedly, when we simply let go. Hans, a friend, says life has taught him this lesson several times.

When I was about twenty-four I began to wake up each morning with a bloody tongue, for no obvious reason. A perceptive family doctor arranged for a friend to watch me while I slept, and he witnessed seizures. I was working in construction, supervising the building of a large apartment house. Suddenly, I had to refocus my whole life. I had been strong and capable, but now I faced multiple restrictions: no driving, no using dangerous machinery, no climbing on roofs or ladders. At first I rebelled against the unfairness of it, but later I came to terms with my limitations and made the best of them. Eventually, anti-convulsant medications even allowed me to drive again.

A few years later I began to work overtime on a regular basis, and being very fatigued, began to have seizures again. Once I was driving a large forklift loaded with cement blocks, and I lost consciousness for several seconds – long enough to drive into a wall and nearly injure another worker. As a new evaluation and new medications were ordered, I was driven to prayer as never before.

During those years I felt drawn to the woman who is now my wife. For a variety of reasons our love was frustrated for more than three years, and I had to let go of it. Looking back, Heather and I both feel that it was as a result of prayer, and of our decision to lay down our dreams and let God work, that we became engaged and then married.

For ten years we were childless, despite our desire to have children. We tried to adopt a child, but for three years nothing worked out. We contacted one adoption agency after another, attended seminars, and looked into private adoption. We wrote hundreds of letters to priests, doctors, clinics, and hospitals. In 1989 we moved to Germany, where we continued our search for a child. The Berlin Wall had just come down, and we heard of an agency in London that was placing unwanted children from the East Bloc with Western couples. Arrangements were made for us to adopt a five-year-old Romanian girl, Marita, and we were almost on the train to fetch her when the agency told us to bring a camera and other expensive items. We began to smell bribery, possibly even black-market connections. I refused to go. At first Heather found it very difficult to give up the child when we were so close to becoming parents, but in the end she let go of it. A few months later we moved back to the United States.

Only days after we arrived back in New York, at a time when we least expected it and were no longer actively pursuing any leads, we received a phone call from a local hospital. An unwed teen mother had given birth to a girl and did not want to keep her. The doctor knew of our interest in adopting a child, and legal arrangements were begun immediately. We brought our new daughter home when she was three days old and named her Marita, after the Romanian child we never saw.

Recently I went through critical brain surgery for my epilepsy. Twice before the operation I was admitted for observation so that the doctors could identify the origin of my seizures. Because I was off my medications, the seizures I experienced were dreadful. One even threw my shoulder out of joint, so badly that I am still doing physical therapy. Later, during my surgery, Heather suffered long hours of worry, but I was calm. I was at peace because I had finally let go, knowing that whatever happened, God would have his hand in it.

Like Hans, we must all be willing to find a bigger horizon than our personal needs. It is one thing to recognize that we are created beings, but quite another to actively turn to the Creator for his guidance in our daily lives. Without this broader view, it is impossible to come to grips with everything that comes our way. Again and again we need to let go of our opinions, our attempts to control our own life, and then God's plans can have power in our lives.

Steven McDonald, a New York City police officer whose story I told in my book *Why Forgive?*, is paralyzed from the neck down as the result of a gunshot wound. He has a tracheostomy, and a respirator must accompany him wherever he goes.

I know I wouldn't be here today, and we wouldn't be together as a family, if it weren't for prayer. There are days I cannot pray and don't want to pray, and that is because Satan is working on me not to talk to God. But I must find the will to pray, because it's our way of communicating with God, to tell him over and over again that we love him. For years I had thought about going to Ireland, as I am an Irish Catholic and have been concerned about the violence going on over there. I always thought about it in my prayers. And then suddenly this summer, there I was in Ireland.

Lately, a lot of people have stopped believing in God. I am able to find strength to survive each day, and to make it from one week to the next only with God's help. People wonder why God allows terrible things to happen on earth. I don't believe God allows bad things to happen, also not to me. Even in a condition like mine, you can be productive for God. I have had to ask myself: How can you live to please God rather than yourself? The answer is to live your life according to God's will. And you need prayer to do that.

Prayer is something we do in *our* time, but the answers come in *God's* time. Sometimes those answers come when we least expect them.

There have been times when I have been very low, times when I have even wanted to kill myself. One time I was feeling terrible and things were just getting to me. My wife, Patti Ann, called Cardinal O'Connor, and he came to our house. One of the things he said was, "Your life can be a prayer." That makes a lot of sense to me.

For years now, Steven has been totally dependent on his wife and his nurses for his twenty-four hour care. But instead of being bitter he radiates peace, and at every opportunity he witnesses to the power of forgiveness and the power of prayer. There is a deep love between husband and wife. Patti Ann is a key player in who Steven is today, and she has been an immeasurable support to him, often acting quietly behind the scenes:

After Steven was shot, it didn't really sink in until the next day that he was seriously injured. I remember coming home from the hospital and saying, "Either go with it, or fight it; either accept it, or blame God." I decided right then to be there for Steven, and to hope and pray. We have our good days and bad days, but prayer is really the only thing we have to hang on to. We are very blessed that we have each other, and through it all we have hung on because of everything that's been given to us. I see other women who have able-bodied husbands and everything they could possibly want, but I wonder if they are satisfied inside.

One reason that prayer might seem so ineffectual in many lives is our refusal to let go and trust in God's leading. How many people are overly concerned about their physical ailments? How many parents obsess over children whom they feel have gone bad ways? Hard as it is, each of us needs to accept the fact that there is a time when we must simply let go of our problems and entrust them to God.

Monica, the mother of Saint Augustine, lived in Hippo (a Roman city in northern Africa) during the fourth century. Her young son, as yet unconverted, lived a life of depravity and sin. In desperation over her son's waywardness, she went to her bishop. His advice? "Stop talking to your son about God. Talk instead to God about your son."

And then there are Jesus' words: "Look at the birds of the air: they neither sow nor reap nor gather into barns, yet your heavenly father feeds them. Are you not more valuable than they? Which of you can add to the value of your life by worrying?"

The death of a child, a devastating illness or debility — these are major events to be sure; but even at such times in life, we must let go. Obviously, one cannot merely abandon significant concerns, but when they loom greater than God, who is the only one who has the power to help us, then our preoccupation becomes self-centered. Merrill, a pastor who worked with me until his death, put it this way: it is a matter of aligning our will with God's will, not the other way around.

When Reseph and Susan, a couple in my church, were expecting their fifth child, they found themselves face to face with this challenge.

Before Daniel was born we knew he would be a very sick little boy – if he made it into the world at all. Halfway through Susan's pregnancy Daniel was found to have enlarged kidneys, and this necessitated his birth two months early. His kidneys had not been able to drain properly, which had caused them to be permanently damaged. The premature birth brought with it a number of other difficulties, and Daniel was attached to many different machines to keep him alive. Several operations had to be done in the first weeks. It was all very difficult for us, and we had to struggle to accept his situation. Why didn't we have a normal child? What happens when our will is different from God's will?

After ten days, when things were looking like Daniel would not pull through, our minister and his wife asked us if we had ever held our little boy in our arms. We had not. So we told the neonatal ICU staff of our wish to take Daniel down to the hospital chapel, where we wanted to hold him and intercede for him.

That same evening, Daniel was brought to the chapel, where a whole crowd of children and adults from our church sang and prayed for our son. Taking him out of the ICU was a bold step, and we didn't know if he'd survive. Every breath had to be pumped into him by hand, and we wept to see him so helpless.

The next morning Daniel seemed much brighter to us, and the nurses showed us that his chart documented a very real improvement. There were several more ups and downs in the following days, but Daniel had definitely turned a corner. After sixty days in the ICU, we could finally bring him home.

Over the next two years, Daniel suffered innumerable complications: infections, operations, more hospitalizations. His parents had to let go of him time and again. They found that whenever they became over-anxious, protective, or hovering, things did not go well – for them or for Daniel. His father writes:

> Those were hard years, caring for such a sick child and our four other young children. We were often exhausted, and would become impatient with our other children.
>
> For the first two years of his life, we were totally preoccupied with Daniel, his needs, his health. Susan was not available, physically or emotionally, for anything else. Then, in the fall of that year, we collapsed. Our minister and his wife spent much time and effort with us, helping us to understand the critical importance of entrusting Daniel completely to God. For the first time, we understood what letting go meant. And so we did it. Miraculously, just as we had been told, God took over in Daniel's little life as never before. He grew and became strong, and he has not been hospitalized since.

12.

remorse

Go tell it on the mountain,
Over the hills and everywhere,
Go tell it on the mountain,
That Jesus Christ is born.

When I was a sinner,
I prayed both night and day.
I asked my Lord to help me,
And he showed me the way.

When I was a seeker,
I sought both night and day.
I asked my Lord to help me,
And he taught me to pray.

He made me a watchman
Upon the city wall;
And if I am a Christian,
I am the least of all.

Traditional Spiritual

One of my favorite songs, "Go tell it on the mountain," contains a remarkably deep understanding of a person's relationship to God. First, the speaker is conscious of his sin; he persists in prayer, pleading for divine intervention, and God answers. But then, like the rest of us, he strays and loses the way. He has to seek it again, diligently, and is led back to prayer, and through it to humility.

We have all done wrong, and many of life's struggles are caused by wrongdoing of one sort or another. Countless people have come to me, burdened by sin and guilt and longing to be freed through confession. When a person comes in a spirit of true remorse, it is a humbling experience. Sometimes my own heart is struck by a confession because I realize I am guilty of the same thing.

Earlier, I mentioned unconfessed personal guilt as a common obstacle to prayer. Though I believe it is a universal truth, it is not universally acknowledged. William Shakespeare recognized it: after Claudius kills his brother, Hamlet's father, to win the crown and the queen, he is shown wrestling with his inability to pray, despite his desire for repentance:

> O, my offense is rank, it smells to heaven;
> It hath the primal eldest curse upon't,
> A brother's murder. Pray can I not,
> Though inclination be as sharp as will:
> My stronger guilt defeats my strong intent;
> And, like a man to double business bound,
> I stand in pause where I shall first begin...
> But, Oh, what form of prayer
> Can serve my turn? 'Forgive me my foul murder'?
> That cannot be; since I am still possess'd
> Of those effects for which I did the murder,
> My crown, mine own ambition and my queen.
> May one be pardon'd and retain the offense?...
> Try what repentance can: what can it not?
> Yet what can it when one can not repent?
> O wretched state! O bosom black as death!

O limed soul, that, struggling to be free,
Art more engaged! Help, angels! Make assay!

In each person is the longing to be in touch with God. Often, however, it is hidden under so many layers of self that the outer life completely masks the inner. In such cases the spiritual life is not even evident; it lies dormant, its potential completely unrealized. Once a spiritual awakening is given, the struggle to remain faithful to that calling begins. This calls for a constant choosing between right and wrong, good and evil, and an ongoing cleansing of ourselves when we make the wrong choice.

Stephanie, a friend living in a neighboring town, wrote to me recently about her many years of searching for truth and meaning in life.

> I had an idyllic childhood in a Jewish home; I was an adored firstborn, a pampered first grandchild on both sides. One relative tried to convince me that I would grow up to be the first woman president, and another that I would become a rich and famous doctor, not to mention stunningly beautiful and well married with a dozen cherubic children.

> I was displayed at weddings and bar mitzvahs and basked in the limelight of it all. We enjoyed huge family gatherings and trips up and down the East Coast. My mother taught me to cook and let me help her prepare for dinner parties even when I needed to stand on a chair to reach the counter. Later, I was given private harp lessons, attended Hebrew school, went on holidays to Cape Cod.

> Four more siblings came along, my father became ill, his business collapsed, and our world changed dramatically by the time I was twelve. But I still expected as much of my

parents' affection and attentions as I had when I was three. I was decidedly self-centered, proud, rebellious, demanding. Some people simply call it "adolescence."

However, I was not yet able to articulate what was troubling me. I had been loved, yet spoiled, and I had few inner resources to draw upon. Then greater issues widened the gap between my parents and me.

As a troubled teenager I sought answers to my problems in the spirit of the early sixties, while on the other side were the enormous spiritual questions that I tried desperately to answer. I wanted to *know*. I wanted to know what I was supposed to do with my life, my destiny. I wanted to know with certainty who is God. I wanted truth.

In this dilemma I began to pray. I asked my parents about prayer, but did not find many answers there. My mother felt that religion was a matter of superstitions lived out of fear by an older, uneducated generation, a crutch to help one in hard times. The inner life was not a priority in my parents' lives.

Over the next few years I visited many different churches but was always disappointed. I was frustrated, disillusioned, and felt my parents were beyond my reach. I actually despaired of ever realizing the truth I had once longed for. I prayed to God from the depths of my despair. I asked him to find some way for me to run away so that life would be happy ever after. But meanwhile my rebellion intensified and so did my despair. Then I prayed that God would take me to heaven and end my misery on earth. I longed to end my torment and knew there was a God who cared, even when no one here below seemed to. I cut my wrists twelve times with a razor.

On the advice of a team of psychiatrists and social workers, my parents reluctantly placed me in a state mental hospital. I was thirteen. I never saw those psychiatrists or social workers again. We were warehoused, building by building, by age, and drugged with huge doses of liquid thorazine into manageable groups. All of the nurses were black and made no secret of hating white people. There were only three white girls in my ward, and the nurses would periodically provoke one of us by stealing a toy or calling us names, and then they would give us an extra shot to "calm" us down.

Only four of the patients could write. I was one of them. I spent my days writing letters for the other 196 girls. Love letters, promises of gang revenge, letters to a parent to rescue their daughter from this hell. One of the girls spent most of her time training the retarded ones to hold their pills under their tongues when they were dispensed and then head for the showers and give them to her. She collected pills that way for a month and then took all of them. We never saw Cynthia again. Another girl, Mary, was there because her mother had tried to poison her, and when the courts incarcerated the mother, she had nowhere to go. Mary was justifiably depressed: all she had to look forward to in life was reaching her eighteenth birthday and being transferred to Building #26, where the women were.

Our fenced day-yard was adjacent to the women's. I was curious to know who all those women were and talked to them whenever I had time outdoors. Some were older, forcibly retired prostitutes. Others had repeatedly tried to take their lives. One younger woman was continually on LSD.

Months melted into years, and I lost all track of time. I first read the Bible in the quiet of a shower stall at that place. I also observed that very few of the girls in Building #36 were actually dangerous, delinquent, incorrigible, or even mentally ill. They were simply unwanted and unloved. Many had never known love.

I am one of the too few survivors of that infamous institution. After my eventual discharge, I refused to return to school. In human terms, life became my teacher, but I know now—it was grace. Over the next few years, I began to ask, Who is this God who saves me? Is it I who am seeking, or, rather, is it he who draws me?

I was not certain then which way to turn. At this time I met a Quaker family who lived near the same college where my father taught. They invited me often, and I found a haven of peace and unconditional love there. I know they prayed for me then, and I am sure they have never stopped. I spent much time in silent prayer and read every religious and theological book that our local library and the university had to offer, and then went to the local parish to ask for baptism. An old Polish priest sat me down in his study to question my motives. He did not ask me about my past, and I took the gospel at its word that I would become a new creature in Christ. I never spoke about the past. I could never forget, but I looked on it as my secret. I was resigned to carry it alone the rest of my life.

My priest was not sure how to avoid the usual ecclesiastical red tape, so he quietly baptized me early one spring morning. No sponsors, no witnesses. He became a "co-conspirator" and a loving grandfather to me.

Once I was convinced that God wanted me, I decided to give my life to him in earnest. I knew I could never return to any semblance of life as I had previously known it. I trusted that I would be led and was, in fact, led sooner than I anticipated. Determined to find a niche somewhere in a religious order, I found a little group of reformed Carmelites. While I was preparing to enter, Reverend Mother arranged for me to meet a friend of hers, a young man recently returned home from a visit to the Trappist monks...

David and I have been married over 30 years. Our marriage has gone through decidedly rocky times, but it has been restored through prayer. Daily we ask each other's forgiveness where we have been impatient, unloving, or selfish. God has sent us many blessings, including five children.

I have seen miracles in the lives of those around me, as well as in my own life. I carried around my past, my horrible secrets, for three decades and now have been able to share all of it with my husband and with our pastor and his wife. I have found a clear conscience and a freeing that I never expected in this world. All of these are miracles, all are undeserved.

Stephanie's story demonstrates several aspects of suffering, communicating with God, and the gift of redemption. But she emphasizes the role of confession: it brought her to a turning point in her life.

Contrition begins with sorrow and grief at our wrongdoing, but it cannot stop there. King David of ancient Israel cried out, "Have mercy upon me!" Tearing one's clothes and dressing in sackcloth, so frequently mentioned in the Bible, are perhaps culturally determined. But the lamentation, weeping, and fasting are more than symbolic; even today these can be outer signs of deep repentance. God wants a change of heart, and true remorse involves both honesty and humility. This will include confession, despite the fact that many Christians today doubt the necessity of confiding one's failures to another person. I believe, however, that the power of sin cannot be broken unless it is exposed in all its blackness. Only then follow forgiveness and a freeing for the soul.

Thérèse de Lisieux uncovers in Scripture a new view of the reality of God's merciful love:

Yes, I feel it; even though I had on my conscience all the sins that can be committed, I would go, my heart broken with sorrow, and throw myself into Jesus' arms, for I know how much he loves the prodigal child who returns to him. It is not because God, in his anticipating mercy, has preserved my soul from mortal sin that I go to him with confidence and love.

All our efforts and striving will not bring repentance; it requires an attitude of remorse and complete surrender to God's working in our lives. My father said there are secrets that only God, in his great love, knows. To this belongs the mystery of repentance. Dostoyevsky expresses this powerfully in *The Brothers Karamazov,* through Father Zossima, a Christ-like figure.

> The elder [Father Zossima] had already noticed in the crowd two glowing eyes fixed upon him. An exhausted, consumptive-looking, though young, peasant woman was gazing at him in silence. Her eyes besought him, but she seemed afraid to approach.
>
> "What is it, my child?"
>
> "Absolve my soul, Father," she articulated softly and slowly, sank on her knees and bowed down at his feet. "I have sinned, Father. I am afraid of my sin."
>
> The elder sat down on the lower step. The woman crept closer to him, still on her knees.
>
> "I am a widow these three years," she began in a half-whisper, with a sort of shudder. "I had a hard life with my husband. He was an old man. He used to beat me cruelly. He lay ill; I thought looking at him, if he were to get well, if he were to get up again, what then? And then the thought came to me—"

"Stay!" said the elder, and he put his ear close to her lips.

The woman went on in a low whisper, so that it was almost impossible to catch anything. She had soon done.

"Three years ago?" asked the elder.

"Three years. At first I didn't think about it, but now I've begun to be ill, and the thought never leaves me."

"Have you come from far?"

"Over three hundred miles away."

"Have you told it in confession?"

"I have confessed it. Twice I have confessed it."

"Have you been admitted to Communion?"

"Yes. I am afraid. I am afraid to die."

"Fear nothing and never be afraid; and don't fret. If only your penitence fail not, God will forgive all. There is no sin, and there can be no sin on all the earth, which the Lord will not forgive to the truly repentant! Man cannot commit a sin so great as to exhaust the infinite love of God. Can there be a sin that would exceed the love of God? Think only of repentance, continual repentance, but dismiss fear altogether. Believe that God loves you as you cannot conceive; that he loves you with your sin, in your sin. It has been said of old that over one repentant sinner there is more joy in heaven than over ten righteous men.

"Go, and fear not. Be not bitter against men. Be not angry if you are wronged. Forgive the dead man in your heart what wrong he did you. Be reconciled with him in truth. If you are penitent, you love. And if you love, you are of God. All things are atoned for, all things are saved by love. If I, a sinner even as you are, am tender with you and have pity on you, how much more will God. Love is such a priceless treasure that you can redeem the whole world by it, and expiate not only your own sins but the sins of others."

Jerome, the fourth-century scholar and Bible trans-
lator, lived in Rome, spent time as an ascetic in the desert,
and founded a school and monastery in Bethlehem. Near the
end of his long life, he wrote down the following conversation, a touching story of what God has done, and continues
to do, for each one of us.

As often as I look at the place where the Lord is born, my
heart enters into a wondrous conversation with the Child
Jesus:

And I say, "Dear Lord Jesus, how you are shivering;
how hard you lie for my sake, for the sake of my redemption. How can I repay you?"

Then I seem to hear the Child's answer: "Dear Jerome,
I desire nothing but that you shall sing 'Glory to God in
the highest,' and be content. I shall be even poorer in the
Garden of Olives and on the Holy Cross."

I speak again, "Dear Jesus, I have to give you something. I will give you all my money."

The Child answers, "Heaven and earth already belong
to me. I do not need your money; give it to the poor, and I
will accept it as if it were given to me."

Then I say, "Dear Jesus, I will gladly do so, but I have to
give something to you personally, or I would die of grief."

The Child answers, "Dear Jerome, since you are so very
generous, I will tell you what you should give me. Give
me your sins, your bad conscience, and those things that
condemn you."

I reply, "What will you do with them?"

The Child says, "I will carry them upon my shoulders;
that shall be my sovereignty and glorious deed. I will bear
your sin and take it away."

Then I begin to weep bitter tears and say, "Little Child,
dear little Child, how deeply you have touched my heart.

I thought you wanted my good deeds, but you want all my evil deeds. Take what is mine, give to me what is thine. So I shall be free from sin and certain of eternal life."

13.

protection

In the summer of 1992 a group of schoolchildren from my community went up to a swimming hole in the Catskills, a popular place for decades. On this day, as usual, some of the children were relaxing in the sun on the rocks. Two girls were on a favorite rock ledge above the pool, and others were still swimming below. Suddenly there was a thunderous crash. The entire ledge had fallen, throwing the girls out into the pool and narrowly missing a boy below, who suffered only a minor injury to his foot. Had the ledge fallen seconds earlier, the boy would have been crushed beneath the rock. If it had collapsed at a different angle, the girls would surely have been pinned between it and the rock wall from which it had broken off. As a shaken teacher put it: "Absolute protection from absolute disaster!"

We pray for many things, but perhaps never as intensely as when our loved ones or we ourselves face physical harm from illness or injury. When protection or healing is granted, a sense of deep gratefulness fills us. When it is not given, however, the pain of the experience may remain as an ineradicable memory.

Clare, a woman who moved to our community several years ago, recalls how she felt when she heard of our church's intercession for two members, both fathers of large families, who were killed in a plane crash.

I was deeply struck upon hearing how the community had gathered on the night they were missing and prayed earnestly for them, not just once, but three times that night. The whole community was really praying for something to happen and expecting God to answer them. It was not play-acting at being Christians; it was the real thing. They were wringing their hearts out before God. That hit me. Since then I've learned of other times of crisis when people will gather quietly to pray around the clock, not heroically, but earnestly carrying a situation on their hearts and interceding for someone in trouble.

Franzi was one of my teachers in grade school, and I loved her dearly, even though she was very strict. Though a tiny, unassuming woman, Franzi had a most dramatic life story, and over the eighty-seven years of her long life she was repeatedly protected in unexpected ways.

Born in Vienna in 1911 to non-religious Jews, Franzi was six when her mother died; her father died the following year. An aunt became guardian of Franzi and her two sisters. The First World War was just over and Vienna was under a blockade. Starvation was imminent, so thousands of children were sent by train across Europe to Sweden, Franzi among them. She was so small and weak that, although seven, she could be carried on one arm. She was in Sweden for two years, and then returned to Austria.

In the mid-1920s anti-Semitism was already strong in the country, and it was only through her aunt's special connections that Franzi was admitted into a teacher's training program. Later she studied philosophy and liberal arts at the University of Vienna, where she met and worked with Edith Stein and Simone Weil, among others. Franzi received her doctorate in May 1937. Her choice for a dissertation, *Poetry of Austrian Workers*, was significant; though an intellectual, she had a deep concern for the working class.

Hitler marched into Austria on March 13, 1938, and life became very hard for all Jews. It was dangerous for an Aryan to be associated with a Jew in any way, but my large circle of non-Jewish friends hid me in their midst and in several cases even risked their lives on my behalf. But then, on November 9, 1938, came the *Kristallnacht,* the "night of broken glass," when Jewish businesses and synagogues throughout the Reich were systematically vandalized, burned, and looted. I too was turned out of my house and onto the street. Fortunately, I had somewhere to go temporarily, but when I returned to my house and asked to have the keys back, I was forced to sign a paper saying that I had left the house because it was in an area where Jews were not allowed to live. So I had to get myself a little room in the Jewish ghetto.

My friends felt sure that war would come, and then I would no longer be able to get out of the country, so at their urging, I left Vienna in April 1939. I didn't have too much trouble getting out of Austria; the difficulty was that England would not accept any Jews from the Continent unless someone in Britain would provide an affidavit, a guarantee for a home and a job. Obtaining such an affidavit had become a life-and-death question for Jews wanting to get out of the Reich; when meeting in the street or anywhere, they would inquire of one another, "Have you got an affidavit yet?"

Aunt Else, my guardian, had been the tutor for Sig-
mund Freud's children, and we were often at their house.
I was especially close to his daughter Anna, although she
was considerably older than I. The Freuds had emigrated
to England the previous year, but Anna had promised she
would help to get me out of Austria. So she signed the
papers on my behalf, and I soon found myself in London
with a place to stay and work as a governess.

Now I was in a foreign country, without money or rela-
tions. Everything was different—language, customs, food,
and political views. Over the next three years I was very
lonely, partly because the English did not look kindly on
"enemy aliens." In Vienna I had thought that to be a Jew
was the worst possible thing, and now I was not only a Jew,
but I was a German Jew. Soon I left my teaching post and
began to work in the Land Army, a corps of manual labor-
ers organized to increase the country's food production.
Once, on a new farm, the owners became suspicious of
me when they found that I was highly educated, and they
reported me as being a spy. Fortunately, nothing came of it.

In my childhood my mother had taught me simple
prayers, and my beloved aunt Else certainly believed in
God. In 1941 I was living with a pastor and his wife, and I
began to read the Bible. I soon felt an immense hunger for
the realization of Christ's teachings on earth. During Lent
1942 I wrote an article for a magazine, "National Socialism:
Not a National but an Individual Problem." Through that
article I was led into contact with the Bruderhof people,
who had fled Hitler's Germany only a few years earlier.

Through all of this, Franzi held firm to her belief in God.
She once told me that despite the horrors of those years,
she never lost faith. She did, however, lose nearly all of her
relatives; they were sent by train to an unknown destination
(Auschwitz?) in Poland.

I had experienced so many miracles of protection. I felt
the need to be forgiven and to forgive. There were times
of great anguish, loneliness, pain, and forsakenness. Yet
the wonder of God's grace has overshadowed everything
for me. He helped me through every need and showed me
again and again that the power of love can overcome all
hatred and evil.

Franzi's escape from certain death at the hands of the Nazis
was always a mystery to her. Why had God let her live,
when so many millions of others had been killed? One thing
was clear to her, however. She felt her life must become an
offering of thanks, both to the God who had protected and
saved her, and to the many who had helped her in times of
danger. And in fact, Franzi did devote the rest of her life
to serving others. Whether to the hundreds of children she
went on to teach over the next decades, or to those who
simply knew her as a neighbor and friend, she will not be
soon forgotten.

Those who follow God conscientiously find that life is
never free of trials, suffering, and even persecution. Only
three years after the Bruderhof settled safely in England, the
British government announced plans to intern all Germans
in camps for "enemy aliens." Because we did not want to
split the community along national lines, we had to find a
new home. Paraguay was the only country open to a large
international group of communal pacifists. John, a Lon-
doner who had joined the community in 1940, remembers:

> Over a sixteen-month period, between November 1940 and
> February 1942, our community members and children trav-
> eled across the Atlantic Ocean, heading to South America.

It was wartime, and travel took a full three weeks because our boats had to zigzag northward, to avoid the usual shipping routes. Three hundred and thirty-eight souls left England in nine separate trips, all under heavy threat of bombing and orders of blackout after dusk.

We knew that many British ships had been sunk by the Axis bombers as well as by U-boats, German surface raiders, and pocket battleships. In spite of the danger of those times, we had faith that God would protect us and bring us to our new home. It was also our faith in the steadfastness of our calling that led us to go ahead. I do not remember much in the way of prayer for our own safety, because we were so concerned for those who remained behind under threat of air raids in England and the war on the Continent. Those still remaining in England interceded on our behalf, I know, and had to put their trust in God as they waited impatiently for news that we had arrived safely at our destination. Later we found out that every one of the Blue Star liners that we traveled out on was sunk in the latter half of 1942 on their way back to Europe.

Arnold and Gladys, fellow Bruderhof members who crossed the Atlantic with their children in the period described by John, recall the complete helplessness they felt on the ship, and an utter dependence on prayer as the sole way to cope.

We were told that if our ship was torpedoed, it would tilt to one side, and that the lifeboats might get hopelessly jammed. If this happened, and the lifeboats could not be thrown into the water, the only hope of survival would be to jump off the ship and try to swim away from it before being sucked down beneath it.

Then, on a practice drill, our cabin steward explained to Gladys that in the event of any trouble with the lifeboats, she was to throw our children over the railing, as far out from the ship as possible. Each child would be given a little life jacket with a red and green light that would go on as soon as it got wet. Theoretically, lifeboats would then come to the rescue. But can you imagine how a mother would feel, being told to throw her baby overboard?

Freda is a Briton who moved to Germany in 1934 to join our community. She recalls:

> The first years of my life in community were particularly stressful, outwardly, inwardly, and politically. Living under the shadow of Hitler's regime meant continual harassment and doubt as to what would happen to us all. Eberhard Arnold was our spiritual leader, and his sudden death in 1935 left the community rudderless. I was fearful, but I never doubted the cause for which I had given my life.
>
> Prayer had always been important for me, but through several events in 1940 and 1941 my faith was severely tested. I had been back in England for two years when a fellow community member, Gertrud, died. She left her husband August a widower and their three little boys without a mother. The next year August asked me to marry him and be a mother to his children. It was only through prayer that I found the firm assurance and joy that this was God's will for me.
>
> Little did I know that a week after our marriage, in May 1940, I would be arrested and interned at an unknown destination. As a result of marrying a German, I had become an enemy alien. As I was being taken away, the police permitted the community to meet for my farewell, and they prayed for my protection. From the moment I was apprehended, I knew I was in God's hands and could trust in him. This never left me during the entire six weeks of my internment on the Isle of Man.

The brothers worked hard for my release, and upon my return home I found the Bruderhof in the midst of packing for emigration to South America. None of us knew what lay ahead, but again I was filled with an absolute trust that God was with us. This certainty prevailed over the fear of the unknown. February 1941 found us embarking, and nine days later, during a storm in the submarine-infested Atlantic, my first child was born.

Through eighteen grueling hours of labor I prayed for strength to carry me through the ordeal. I never doubted in God's protection for myself and my child. The ship's doctor, who had not delivered a baby for fifteen years, had to contend with the violent pitching of the ship, the port-hole flying open, and his instruments being dashed to the floor. All one hundred and fifty men, women, and children from the community who were on board the ship, as well as the entire crew, celebrated the birth of our daughter, and the crew saw it as a good omen foretelling a safe arrival at our destination. I knew God would preserve us, but there must have been an underlying fear in me, because shortly after the baby's birth I had a most vivid dream that our ship had been torpedoed and my baby was drowning before my eyes. Trust in God and joy in my child, however, prevailed in my waking hours.

14.

selflessness

There is a story about a rabbi known for his compassion and wisdom who was visited by an angel. The angel said, "I am a messenger of the Lord, sent to bring you a gift from heaven. Ask for anything you want." The angel asked three times, but the rabbi could not think of anything he needed. He thought of money, long life, wisdom, but finally told the angel: "Tell the Lord that I am honored, but he has provided me with so much that there is nothing I lack or am in need of. In fact, there is nothing that I desire. I am content."

Then the angel spoke:

> You are a stupid and selfish man. In your selfishness you refused God's gift. You could have asked for anything! You could have asked for no more hunger or disease or war upon the earth, for no more hatred. You could have asked for the victory of righteousness over injustice. You could have asked for the Messiah to come! And all you could think of was your own miserable life.

To a greater or lesser degree, we are all like the rabbi. Perhaps we lead godly lives and are not willfully selfish, yet daily we pass up opportunities to express our love and caring. At root, we are all egocentric, and this doesn't necessarily stop when we speak to God. Sure, we intercede for the dying friend and the relative gone bad ways, but do we often enough ask God to bless others, or to intervene in their lives? Our prayers will be nothing more than self-serving piety if we ignore the needs of those around us. If we truly love our neighbors, then we will pray for them. Praying in this way — that is, focusing on the needs of others — draws us away from our personal troubles and broadens our horizons.

Christ admonished us to make peace with our brother before we bring our offering to God, that is, before we pray with one another. This is not just an illustration, but like the Lord's Prayer, it actually points to God's justice: we will be forgiven only to the degree that we forgive others. We expect others to forget the wrongs we have done them, yet cling to our own petty grudges, to our hatred, and the injustices done to us. One of the most difficult words of Jesus to put into practice is about loving our enemies and praying for those who persecute us. Certainly this does not mean we must condone the evil they perpetrate, but we are called to love them.

We also cannot demonize a specific person, no matter what evil he has done. Many people would have us think of Hitler as a devil, but I am not sure it helps anyone to label even such a godless man in this way. If we hate someone, it will not be long before we are also capable of killing him, for "he who hates his brother is a murderer." Our love must know no bounds; whoever it is, it makes no difference to whom we offer our love.

To one who blames Hitler

We – all of us – bear our guilt;
Like rainfall – we are together – and the flood
Comes from our separate strength.
Therefore this hate is not on him,
Not wholly born of his peculiar gall
Which writhes the world with pain.
I have seen your eyes flash with hate;
My friend, the serpent lurks within you, too.
Your venom coils and waits.

Jane Tyson Clement

In Nazi Germany in the 1930s, my grandfather felt an urge to make public his refusal to have anything to do with the country's new policies of bigotry, racism, and nationalism. He wrote directly to Hitler, challenging him about the violations of morality, family life, justice, the common good, and truth. In spite of the evil spirit the Nazis represented, my grandfather prayed unceasingly that God would intervene and change their hearts.

We intercede for all people, for we wish that everyone may be drawn into the powerful happenings of the coming of God and his future kingdom. In our prayer we include all our relatives, all friends and enemies, for we are urged to this by God's love. Jesus himself prayed for the authorities who brought him to his death, "Father, forgive them, for they know not what they do." When we pray for the hostile authorities in the same way as for our hearts' dearest friends, we are asking for the Holy Spirit to come down, to visit our beloved friends and enemies wherever they may be, and to touch and move their hearts in whatever condition they may be.

Further, my grandfather believed that we must not only love and intercede for our enemies, but we must pray that we have faith and understanding for them, that "in spite of their blindness, they see the wrong they are doing, and that the divine ember in each of them is fanned into a flame." In July 1935 he had a dream:

> Last night Hitler appeared to me in a dream. I had painted a picture, and he was trying to paint over it, saying he could do it better. He then sat down and I said to him, "My dear Adolf, this cannot continue much longer. Even you yourself cannot be enjoying this killing anymore." Then he asked me what I thought about war. I answered, "We must hold firmly to love and nonviolence, for killing is against love in every situation."
>
> Hitler became very angry. But the wonderful thing about the dream was that I had a heart-to-heart talk with him. I was not in the least afraid...
>
> Perhaps one day this dream will be fulfilled. But it must be our concern that our love, also to those who hate us, finds such expression that we reach their hearts. For that is what love is. If we reach the heart of a person, we will find the hidden spark from God, even if he is the greatest criminal. Forgiveness must become a reality.

Of course, my grandfather was not alone in this attitude; many throughout history have shared his belief in the power of an all-encompassing love, even for the most depraved person. I have heard that A.J. Muste, the well-known peace activist, used to say during World War II, "If I cannot love Hitler, I am not a Christian." And Michael Henderson, author of several books on peace and forgiveness, wrote regarding his prayers for Hitler: "I don't think it had any effect on him, but it certainly did on me. I felt that all hate and bitterness against the Germans had vanished…"

Recently I became aware of a remarkable prayer, found on a piece of old wrapping paper in Ravensbrück (a Nazi concentration camp for women) after the war:

> Lord, remember not only the men and women of good will, but also those of ill will. But do not remember all the suffering they have inflicted upon us. Remember the fruits we brought, thanks to this suffering: our comradeship, our loyalty, our humility, the courage, the generosity, the greatness of heart that has grown out of this. And when they come to judgment, let all the fruits we have borne be their forgiveness.

Else, my great-aunt, died of tuberculosis in 1932. The disease was rampant in Europe in those years and took its toll particularly among the poor and undernourished. It was called "consumption," for it literally consumed the person from the inside out. Nothing was available in the way of medical treatment, although rest and good nutrition were known to be helpful, and clean fresh air was certainly beneficial. In 1922 Else's sister Olga had died from tuberculosis of the lungs. A few years later, Else herself became tubercular. In 1929 the doctors told her she had only days left to live. After intense prayer by the whole community on her behalf, she recovered, to the point that she could adopt and care for a little orphan boy.

My father described Else as a loving, simple, and humble person. She was completely selfless and dedicated to her work, which consisted primarily of research and secretarial work for my grandfather. Her days were spent in service to others, and no matter how busy she was, she always had time to talk with someone, especially those who came to her with their troubles. Though Papa was only eighteen when his aunt Else died (she was in her forties), they were close friends, and she often confided in him. Else told him, "It should be our prayer to be made usable for the kingdom of God, not for our own sakes but for the sake of others." For her, the greatest thing in God was his mercy and forgiveness, and the fact that his peace is there for everyone. She often reminded those around her of Christ's wonderful words, "Be not afraid: I have overcome the world," which she saw as a powerful encouragement to anyone tormented by fear or anxiety for the future.

Else believed that faith alone could free one from the fear of death. She knew what she was talking about. In her last weeks she had high fevers and felt miserable. She vomited a lot and had uncontrollable fits of coughing. Even during those days and nights of intense suffering, Else did not think of herself. Her longing and prayer was to surrender everything so that God's power would be visible on earth and the hearts of people touched and changed through this. She often spoke of God's greatness and of the great things he would bring about in the future.

Like everyone else, Else had weaknesses. What made her different was her selflessness and her firm belief in the nearness of God. She once expressed the desire to die with her hands reaching up to heaven, and when asked what her greatest wish was, she said, "Only to love others more."

15.

service

As unassuming as Mother Teresa was, something of God unquestionably radiated from her. She showed her love in deeds; that is what made her words significant.

Everything in her life was an expression of prayer – her scolding, her humor, her example of serving the poor instead of preaching about it. Her work continues to inspire people all over the world, making the promise in Revelation a reality: "Blessed are they who die in the Lord, for their works shall follow after them."

Once someone asked Mother Teresa where she found the strength for the enormous work she did for the poor. Her answer:

> My secret is quite simple – I pray! You should spend at least half an hour in the morning and an hour at night in prayer. You can pray while you work. Work doesn't stop prayer, and prayer doesn't stop work. It requires only that small raising of mind to him: "I love you, God, I trust you, I believe in you, I need you now." Small things like that. They are wonderful prayers.

Prayer cannot be an excuse for inaction. Love must be put into deeds. As writer Anna Mow used to say, "Love is an action, not a feeling." If we pray for God's will to be done on earth, then our life will be a life of work. For just as faith without works is dead, prayer without work is hypocrisy. Unless our love is expressed in deeds, our spiritual life will wither and die. John Michael Talbot tells us that, for Francis of Assisi, solitude and service were two sides of the same coin. And Dorothy Day said that she believed many people pray not through words but through the witness of their lives, "through the work they do and the love they offer to others."

Each of us can offer to God the things we do during the course of the day. George Arthur Buttrick once wrote that "fields are not plowed by praying over them. But let a man remember that fields become a drudgery, or a botched labor, or even a greed and a bitterness, unless the plowing is done in prayer." There is a difference between just doing something, and making it a prayer. When we make our work a prayer, we do it not only for ourselves or our neighbor, but for God. All our loving deeds, all our work for human justice and the relief of suffering, are not really prayers until self is out of the way, and we acknowledge God and recognize that we are just as much in need of him as he is in need of us to do his works.

For my parents, service was a form of prayer, born out of their conviction that loving thoughts and words must be brought to fruition in concrete deeds. My mother, particularly, could never find enough minutes in the day to do what she wanted in the way of service to others, showing them love, meeting their needs. Both my parents believed and taught us children that a person can use a day the right way or the wrong way, or do nothing at all with that day; but each day gone is one day less that we have to serve. Stephen Grellet writes: "I expect to pass through this world but once: any good thing, therefore, that I can do, or any kindness that

I can show to any fellow creature, let me do it now; let me not defer nor neglect it, for I shall not pass this way again."

Author Dorothy Gauchat, an old friend, dedicated her life to serving disabled children with her husband Bill. To them, Jesus' words, "whatever you do unto the least of them, you do unto me" were not only an observation, but a command.

Living and working with such children in a spirit of compassion and reverence for each child is a service of love; in fact, it is a prayer, because it is an offering to God. It is strenuous and at times tedious work—long days and short nights—but it is rewarding beyond measure. Dorothy writes:

> Over the past fifty years children have been the center of my life—my own children as well as many youngsters with handicaps whose parents for various reasons were unable to care for them. What began in the 1940s as a small hospitality home for children with special needs grew like "the woman who lived in a shoe and had so many children she didn't know what to do." Daily requests came from agencies and hurting parents, begging us to take yet another child. We already had fifteen infants and toddlers, and more requests led us to delve deeply into the needs of special children.
>
> Trips to state institutions where these children were sent revealed the horror of man's inhumanity to man. As I walked from one building to another, I was sickened by the sight of unloved, uncared-for children swarming around like frightened lambs, with outstretched arms begging to be loved.
>
> When we started this work, there were no books or courses on the subject of handicapped children. The result

of our research and the growing knowledge of our pio-neer methods in caring for these children strengthened our conviction that we were called, indeed had the per-sonal responsibility as followers of Christ, to make room for more children. First, with the help of friends and foun-dations, guided by the hand of God, we built an addition to our home, which enabled us to welcome twenty-five more children. Eventually we bought a large house situ-ated on a lovely tract of land with stables where horses had been boarded. The house, named the Croft, became a group home for fifteen young adults who had outgrown the children's home. When our wheelchair-bound children reached the age of eighteen years, another home was built to fit their needs.

Perhaps our example of "love made visible" was respon-sible for touching the hearts of countless generous friends. This was the forerunner of dramatic changes in attitude of the powers controlling the care and destinies of retarded and mentally handicapped children and adults. When community group homes sprang up and state institutions began to release patients, society in general seemed to bet-ter accept folks with special needs.

Six years ago I was present at the birth of my grandson Jonathan. At the invitation of the doctor, I stood between the doctor and nurse to witness this birth. I was transfixed at the awesome sight as the newborn slipped from the safety of his mother's womb into the hands of the doctor. The joy of that moment was turned into sorrow at the sight of the twisted legs of this little boy. I fled from the delivery room, overcome now with grief and anger. Anger with God that he sent a handicapped infant to this young couple, whose father, Todd, was wheelchair-bound with cerebral palsy.

Tears washed over my face as I drove home, demand-ing "Why, God, why? How could you do this to my son and daughter-in-law?" There was little sleep for me that night my grandson was born; the pain of seeing little Jonathan facing limitations in life as his father had was almost unbearable. As dawn broke, a calmness embraced me as though being held by God. He works in mysterious ways. I found myself comforted with the thought that this little boy was sent with a special mission to be a special son. He would truly understand his father's inability to run, speak, walk, or do the active things other young fathers do with their sons. There seemed little doubt that there would be a special bond between father and son. Days later, I caught a glimpse of the infant cradled in the arms of his dad. It seemed to portray a different picture of the Madonna and child. He surely was a gift from God. And eventually, surgeries, casts, and braces enabled Jonathan to walk...

One of hundreds of children who came to join our family was an infant named Anthony. We were told he was blind and deaf. He was hydrocephalic, which means he had severe water pressure on the brain. The water pressure was slightly visible. In a short time, it was apparent that Anthony could both see and hear. To me, he was a beautiful infant with tiny features, a pert little nose, brown hair and bright eyes. He was another child who needed to be loved. It did not take long for our caregivers to fall in love with him, especially his assigned caregiver, Rita. By nature, Rita seemed gruff, opinionated, with a touch of salty impatience toward younger members of our staff. Beneath this crusty shell, however, beat a heart full of tenderness. To me, she was a diamond in the rough. The staff loved and respected her. But the children loved her most of all, especially little Anthony...

I have cared for many handicapped children and adults. Every one of them has touched the lives of countless people: staff, relatives, and friends. They, the children, communicate their love in a mysterious but tangible way. I often came upon folks just holding Anthony's tiny hand, feeling his love, his innocence, flowing from his hand to theirs. In my mind, there has never been a doubt that this precious infant was sent by God to teach us to love and to be loved. We were told that Anthony would not live beyond three years, but love is a powerful elixir. He lived for nine.

Dorothy Day had a great love and respect for the Gauchats and the work they did, and visited them often. Each visit was spiritual refreshment. In her book *On Pilgrimage*, she wrote:

> If I did not believe, if I did not make what is called an act of faith (and each act of faith increases our faith, and our capacity for faith), if I did not have faith that such work as the Gauchats' does lighten the sum total of suffering in the world, so that those who are suffering on both sides of this ghastly struggle somehow mysteriously find their pain lifted and some balm of consolation poured on their wounds, if I did not believe these things, the problem of evil would indeed be overwhelming.

Owen and Alice were a childless couple in their forties who moved to our community in 1943. A fall from a horse left Owen with a permanently stiff knee. He walked with a severe limp and always carried a cane. Alice herself was not the strongest; she had suffered from painful rheumatoid arthritis since her younger years, which became crippling as she grew older. But when, in the aftermath of World War II, the opportunity arose for the community to take in ten German war orphans, the Humphreys eagerly volunteered to serve as houseparents. They welcomed these children into their home with tremendous love and devotion.

Neither Owen nor Alice knew any German, and none of the children spoke English, but as the months went by, they grew together as a real family. Soon three more children were added to their number. The war orphans had been uncared for and lacked any kind of discipline. The Humphreys gathered them, read to them, taught them arts and crafts, worked and played with them, and most of all loved them. They were both teachers, so they were with children all day, but after school they still had their own thirteen children to occupy, bathe, play with, and put to bed.

Years later, when Alice was asked, "How did you ever manage?" she replied, "I prayed all day for guidance and strength. And it was our privilege, our joy!" From a letter Owen wrote to Alice while he was on a trip:

> When I think through the years we have had together, I am deeply happy for what has been given to us. We have not had all that we wished for, and our great desire for children of our own was not granted to us, but we have been given the very great joy of caring for children as though they were our own.

Though every community surely has at least one such dedicated person, not all of us are given the opportunity or the vision, let alone the strength, for great works of mercy. But why should that hinder us from doing what we can? Whenever I think about the meaning of service, Sara, a deceased friend who never seemed to tire of showing kindness to everyone around her, comes to mind.

Life was not easy for Sara, and there were many heartaches along with the joys. Three of her fourteen children were taken from her by disease—one from meningitis, another from diphtheria, and still another from a heart condition. Sara was a capable cook, and she especially enjoyed putting away food for winter: from planting and harvesting to canning and freezing. Even in her seventies, she insisted on gardening alongside her daughters in the family's large vegetable patch. Sara also loved to work with wool, and could be found hour after hour spinning at her wheel. In between she knitted mittens and sweaters for anyone who needed them.

Sara found plenty of small needs that had to be attended to every day: a discouraged neighbor who needed an uplifting word, a sick or housebound person to visit. And yet she was a quiet woman, not a talker but a doer. For her, the most important prayer was simply service.

After Sara died, a small sheet of paper was found in her desk, with words she had laboriously copied out from Mother Teresa:

A few ways to practice humility:
Speak as little as possible of oneself.
Mind your own business.
Avoid curiosity.
Do not want to manage other people's affairs.
Accept contradiction and correction cheerfully.
Pass over the mistakes of others.
Accept blame when innocent.
Yield to the will of others.
Accept insults and injuries.
Accept being slighted, forgotten, and disliked.
Be kind and gentle, even under provocation.
Do not seek to be specially loved and admired.
Never stand on one's dignity.
Choose always the hardest.

Dostoyevsky tells the story of a selfish old woman who died. Her angel went to God and asked how this woman could be saved. God asked the angel if she had ever done a good deed. The angel had to think hard, because she had done very little for others while on earth. But yes, many years ago she had pulled up an onion from her garden and given it to a beggar woman. God told the angel to get that onion and go down to hell, find the woman, and bring her up to heaven. The angel leaned down into hell, and told the woman to catch hold of the onion so he could pull her out. At this, the other sinners in hell, seeing how she was being saved, began clinging on to her. But she was a very possessive woman, and she began kicking them. "*I'm* to be pulled out, not you! It's my onion, not yours." As soon as she said that, the onion broke. She fell back into hell. The angel wept and went away.

To me, this parable says that God will stop at nothing to save a person. And it shows the significance of every self-less deed – in contrast to the strenuousness of a self-centered struggle for spiritual fulfillment. In my grandfather's words, "People who spend all their energy on ensuring their own salvation or keeping their inner life just above water are so preoccupied with themselves that they have no strength left to love."

16.

contemplation

I have always enjoyed fishing. Now, with my children grown and my grandchildren old enough to come with me, I go fishing as often as I can get away. Mostly we just sit in the boat for hours and catch nothing. But those hours of quiet are valuable for thinking. I have pondered how the first disciples Jesus called were fishermen, and how they were obedient when Jesus said, "Leave your nets and come, follow me." And how after the crucifixion the disciples, in their discouragement, returned to the solitude of their fishing boats.

Fishing, like prayer, can bring peace of heart and give time for personal reflection. Like prayer, it can be disheartening – sometimes the catch will be small, or there will be nothing but a few bites. Both fishing and prayer require patience and humility, because with both, you ultimately depend on an answer from outside yourself.

A conversation involves both talking and listening, and as we all know, real listening requires us to become quiet first. What God wants to tell us is of greater importance than what we want to tell him. Writer John Dear, a Jesuit priest and peace activist, recently told me:

> I realized that for many years I had been telling God what
> to do. But God is a living being, and in a relationship of

love, we need to listen to one another. Prayer is a time of listening to God and just being quiet with the one I love. It is entering into a living and loving relationship with God. The listening is important. We have been talking for so long that we need to let God get a word in edgewise, give him a chance to change us.

As much as the physical body requires rest and sleep in order to function properly, so our inner life requires regular times of quiet in which the soul can be strengthened again: "For everything there is a season, and a time for every purpose under heaven: a time to weep, and a time to laugh; a time to mourn, and a time to dance; a time to keep silence, and a time to speak…"

This is true for everybody, but "a time to keep silence" may be most important for people who are actively involved in a cause or service. They will find that strength for their work comes first from the inner springs of their personal spiritual life, and that inner quiet is essential to balancing the busyness of their days.

The story of the prophet Elijah, as told in the Old Testament, has always meant a great deal to me, for although Elijah did many great and wonderful works for God, it is clear that he had his share of human weaknesses. The difference is that he listened and "waited upon God." Through that, his prayers for rain were answered, his prayer to bring a dead child back to life was heeded, and he was given tremendous spiritual power to confront idolatry and false prophecy. And in spite of his low moments, his times of despair, and his doubts about his own fitness for the task, he remained faithful. Once Elijah was in such despair that he begged God to take his life. In response, the Lord told Elijah to go and stand on the mountain, and he sent a strong wind that broke the rocks into pieces, and after that an earthquake, and then a great fire. But the Lord was not to be found in any of these—only in the "still small voice" that followed.

Life seems like a long string of events, planned or unplanned, joyful or sorrowful. As significant as each one appears to be when we stand in its midst, it can often be a distraction that draws our attention away from the larger picture. If we are to communicate with God, we must first become inwardly quiet, detached from our roving thoughts, our worries and fears for tomorrow. It is not without significance that Mother Teresa's "business card" places silence first; it is indeed the prerequisite for all the other gifts of the Spirit:

> The fruit of silence is prayer.
> The fruit of prayer is faith.
> The fruit of faith is love.
> The fruit of love is service.
> The fruit of service is peace.

Just as life demands both thought and action, so there must also be a balance between solitude and community. Outward silence is easily achieved when one is alone, though mind and heart may still be busy; but in true solitude one can often come before God in a way not possible when there is even one other person present.

Communal prayer to God, whether in silence or in speech, must always have its root in the secluded prayer life of each individual believer, for how can a church be strong if the prayer life of its individual members is weak?

Silence can draw a group of believers close together in their common searching and allow God's power to be felt among them. The Quakers, or Society of Friends, have long valued silence as the most direct way to deal with the preoccupations of the mind, so that the still small voice of God can be heard. But outer silence is not sufficient; there must also be inward quietness.

A woman in my church who spent many years with the Quakers describes her experience:

> Several of us met twice weekly in silence to wait on the Spirit. Some meetings yielded wonderful outpourings, but others were just plain dead. It depended on what spirit we were in, and how genuine we were in our hunger for God's truth to expose what lay within our hearts. It took desire and discipline on our part to shut out all of the other things that so easily came to mind as we sat in silence: lists of things to do, items not to be forgotten, projects to be completed...

In our church we have experienced similar meetings where there was little movement of the Spirit. Contemplative prayer is a discipline, and not easily learned. Alan Mermann, writer as well as physician and minister, pinpoints what may be the problem for many of us:

> It takes so little to distract me, no matter how desperate I may be for the focused introspection I imagine true prayer to be. The slightest stimulus from my immediate environment, the silliest thought, or the most insignificant itch can effectively interrupt my efforts. But I am confident that prayer links me with that ubiquitous power, that profound depth of unconscious reality, that endless source of creative energy that I call God.

Inner silence and quiet before God is especially important at times of decision. Jesus knew the value of seclusion; he withdrew from the company of others at several crucial moments in his life: prior to his temptation by Satan, before the transfiguration, and in the garden after his last meal with his disciples. Likewise, we need to take time for reflection and silent prayer, asking God for wisdom and discernment to make the right choices and decisions as we meet the many demands that make up daily life.

All religions of the world contain an element of mysticism, and each has nurtured its own tradition of the mystical life. Essential to all mystical traditions is the belief that the mystic's spiritual journey is undertaken on behalf of all humanity, and that through discipline of the senses, freedom is granted from the physical and temporal, revealing to the soul the true experience of God. My father loved the writings of Meister Eckhardt, the great mystic of the thirteenth century, because they emphasize the heart that listens to God alone. The mystics believe that, rather than intricate liturgies and strict observances, God desires a heart that detaches itself in silence from everything and turns and listens to him, so that he may fill it with his infinite love.

The following poem by Madeleine L'Engle expresses this thought eloquently:

I, who live by words, am wordless when
I try my words in prayer. All language turns
To silence. Prayer will take my words and then
Reveal their emptiness. The stilled voice learns
To hold its peace, to listen with the heart
To silence that is joy, is adoration.

The self is shattered, all words torn apart
In this strange patterned time of contemplation
That, in time, breaks time, breaks words, breaks me,
And then, in silence, leaves me healed and mended.
I leave, returned to language, for I see
Through words, even when all words are ended.
I, who live by words, am wordless when
I turn me to the Word to pray. Amen.

Doris Grumbach, in *The Presence of Absence,* recounts how, as an atheist, she experienced the reality of God, not through anything she did or anything she imagined—it just happened. She was sitting on the steps in front of her home, when she was overcome "with a unique feeling of peace, an impression so intense that it seemed to expand into ineffable joy."

> It went on, second after second, so pervasive that it seemed to fill my entire body. I relaxed into it, luxuriated in it. Then with no warning, and surely without preparation or expectation, I knew what it was: for the seconds it lasted I felt, with a certainty I cannot account for, a sense of the presence of God.

At the time of this experience she was, in her own words, "a young woman without a history of belief, without a formal religion or rather any at all." As a result, she began attending church. Then, after five decades of church-going, she realized she needed something more, and turned to the mystics, the contemplatives. She was tired of form and wanted a spirituality "reduced to nothing, no words, because I had begun to distrust the vehicle of words."

Contemplation, that deep inward concentration of the soul, has often been held up in contrast to the active life of devout service. Yet the two are not mutually exclusive;

indeed, one requires the other. In the New Testament we are told that Mary loved Jesus so much that she simply sat at his feet and adored him, while Martha busied herself with the housework and served the guests. She complained to Jesus about her sister Mary, but he chided her for her worry, and said that Mary had chosen what was better. Too often the Marthas feel that they are accomplishing the good in the world while the Marys merely spend their time in idle meditation. Each has a task in life, although they may be very different, and each task is necessary and has its own purpose in the whole picture.

Regarding contemplation, I have found nothing better than the words of Thomas Merton, monk, mystic, author, and activist:

> The contemplative life is the search for peace not in an abstract exclusion of all outside reality, not in a barren negative closing of the senses upon the world, but in the openness of love. It begins with the acceptance of my own self in my poverty and my nearness to despair in order to recognize that where God is there can be no despair, and God is in me even if I despair…The contemplative is not the man who has fiery visions of the cherubim carrying God in their imagined chariot, but simply he who has risked his mind in the desert beyond language and beyond ideas, where God is encountered in the nakedness of pure trust—that is to say, in the surrender of our poverty and incompleteness in order no longer to clench our minds in a cramp upon themselves, as if thinking made us exist.
>
> The message of hope the contemplative offers you, then, is not that you need to find your way through the jungle of language and problems that today surround God; but that whether you understand or not, God loves you, is present

in you, lives in you, dwells in you, calls you, saves you, and offers you an understanding and light that are like nothing you ever found in books or heard in sermons...If you dare to penetrate your own silence, then you will truly recover the light and the capacity to understand what is beyond words and beyond explanations because it is too close to be explained: it is the intimate union, in the depths of your own heart, of God's spirit and your own secret inmost self.

Over the centuries there have been many who have found their spiritual calling in contemplation, meditation, or mysticism, and out of their experiences, countless techniques to further our spiritual silence have been developed, such as *lectio divina* (spiritual reading), journaling, and various forms of meditation. Though these aids are certainly of value, they should never become an end in themselves. What is of utmost importance is not the spiritual state of the individual in itself, but his attitude – that he is standing in reverence before God.

Much "alternative" religion today focuses on our personal relationship with God, and emphasizes the inner silence of which I have been speaking as a means to attain community with God. Not all of it is "Christian," yet I believe there is still much that can be learned from it. Some time ago I visited a Buddhist commune in France, Plum Village, and though there was no formal prayer as we know it, there was an atmosphere of togetherness, mindful listening to one another, and the recognition that peace and harmony are easily disturbed by too much chatter and bustle.

Many people, disenchanted with institutional religion, go outdoors into nature to satisfy their spiritual needs. There is great inner strength given through the beauty of unspoiled creation, and peace, fresh insights, and wide horizons are certainly of psychological and physical benefit. But it will remain self-deification as long as we remain focused on ourselves and our personal experience, instead of on God. New Age and similar movements are partially attractive because they are non-threatening and demand little from the participant. But a true relationship with God requires energy and commitment, and is often tumultuous, not simply a feel-good phenomenon. Whether we adhere to Christianity, Buddhism, or anything else, we must go beyond the "looks good/feels good" stage to a recognition of God as the creator and redeemer of the earth and skies. The moment we acknowledge God, centering our heart and mind on his power, a spiritual depth can be realized. As John Michael Talbot writes, "All creation bears the traces of its creator and will lead the spiritually sensitive seeker back to God."

One of my nephews has written to me:

> My mind is often so cluttered and conflicted, so noisy, that it must be completely cleared out and silenced. But that is also a preparation for prayer. Recently I have found that talking less (and listening more), watching the sunset, taking time to breathe in fresh air outdoors, or putting my mind and hands to hard physical work – any of these can bring me closer to God. The issue, however, is not me, but God.

In Europe during the first decades of the twentieth century a widespread movement of youth groups formed around the belief that the bourgeois conventions of society should be abandoned in favor of simplicity, sincerity, honest relationships, and love of nature. They hiked in the mountains, played folk music, enjoyed the old circle dances, and in the evening met silently around a fire, which for them was a spiritual experience, the flames flickering on the faces of those gathered, all looking to the center, a symbol of our inner centering on God. My grandmother, an avid participant in this so-called Youth Movement, writes:

> We sensed that hidden in nature lay a mystery: God. Most had not experienced God or had lost sight of him—if not through disillusionment with the established churches, then through the terrible experiences of the First World War. Out in nature, however, we felt something of a true quest for the unknown God—and a sense of great reverence for him—when we gathered and sang together. Behind all this stood a Creator whose name we hardly dared pronounce, it had been so misused and distorted.

Though careful to note the distinction between worshipping creation and worshipping the creator, whose divine Spirit is seen at work in it, my grandfather reveled in the beauty of nature and often expressed himself in verses that are really personal prayers put on paper:

> The valley opens wide,
> Warm sunshine floods the earth with light.
> O may my heart awake to thee,
> Be opened, opened wide,
> That I for thee may be outpoured,
> In stillness now may wait for thee.
>
> My eyes be lifted high
> To view creation's wondrous might,
> To view the wideness of the plains:
> Yea, thou art great! Not I.
> Thou all in all, no separate one,
> In thy creation oneness reigns.

God, thou art great, so great —
To thee the widest land is small.
Thy Spirit is unbounded, free.
We love thee without end.
Surrendered wholly to thy call,
I lose myself, to live in thee.

17.

worship

I often wonder whether we sufficiently grasp or appreciate the tremendous gift of being able to come to God in prayer. As many of the stories I have recounted so far indicate, sorrow and heartache drive most of us to God without a second thought. As for thanking or praising him when things are going well, however, we are often negligent. All the same, I believe that worship must be a part of our prayers. When we have joy in God, we will feel a natural urge to honor him, for we will be unable to forget for even an hour that it is he who protects us, holds us through hard times, provides us with everything we need, and gives us hope for the future, no matter how bleak things may seem.

Take, for example, the following part of a letter written by Etty Hillesum, a Dutch Jew who suffered and died in a Nazi death camp.

You have made me so rich, O God, please let me share your bounty with open hands. My life has become an uninterrupted dialogue with you. Sometimes when I stand in some corner of the camp, my feet planted on your earth, my eyes raised toward your heaven, tears run down my face, tears of deep emotion and gratitude. At night, too, when I lie in my bed and rest in you, O God, tears of gratitude run down my face, and that is my prayer. I have been terribly tired for several days, but that too will pass; things come and go in a deeper rhythm and people must be taught to listen to it. It is the most important thing we have to learn in this life...

I may never become the great artist I would really like to be, but I am already secure in you, God. Sometimes I try my hand at turning out small profundities and uncertain short stories, but I always end up with just one single word: God. And that says everything, and there is no need for anything more.

We have so much to be thankful for, so infinitely much more than Hillesum, yet how often we forget to thank and praise God. And when we think of people in the so-called developing nations, in the hunger-stricken, blood-drenched, devastated parts of this earth, it is clear that most of us have suffered very little in our lives. We are surrounded by peace and plenty. We have no reason and no excuse for ingratitude – as Desmond Tutu calls it, the "deeper leprosy of the spirit." In all my travelling and reading, I have noted that people who really suffer – who live in poverty and unbelievable hardship – are much more thankful than we. Such people, it seems, are continually praising God. Paul instructs us to rejoice in the Lord always, to pray constantly, and to give thanks in all circumstances. The prophet Habakkuk says, "Though the fig tree does not blossom, nor any fruit be on the vines, though the produce of the olive fail, and the fields yield no food, though the flock be cut off from the fold, and there be no herd in the stalls, yet will I rejoice in the Lord, the God of my salvation."

God is so good that he not only accepts our feeble stammering, but desires it. We may be small and weak, but God loves and affirms us in that very smallness. And it is in recognizing that we are unworthy of his care, his love, and his generous gifts, that our gratitude to him is born. Through our faith in him, we come to know what an inexhaustible wealth of grace awaits those who call on God.

> Blessed that flock safe penned in Paradise;
> Blessed this flock that tramps in weary ways;
> All form one flock, God's flock; all yield him praise
> By joy, or pain, still tending toward the prize.
> Joy speaks in praises there, and sings and flies
> Where no night is, exulting all its days;
> Here, pain finds solace, for, behold, it prays;
> In both, love lives the life that never dies.
>
> *Christina Rossetti*

God is spirit, life, movement, and change. Jesus contrasted "the wind that blows where it wills" with established routine, with designated places of worship, with form and structure. Perhaps that is also why Jesus never wrote anything down; he passed everything on to his disciples by word of mouth, so that his message would spread in a living way, from heart to heart, from experience to experience. It is recorded only once that Jesus wrote something, and that was in the sand, where the wind would blow it away. If we are open to the Spirit of God moving in us and around us, we will find ourselves in a worshipful attitude many times every day: upon arising, in our relationships with others, and when we witness the beauty of the world around us.

The early church father Clement of Alexandria expressed his worship in written words that overflow with joy and an unwavering faith.

> O bridle of racing young horses,
> Wing of soaring birds,

Safe rudder of sailing boats,
Shepherd of the royal lambs!
Unite thy simple children
That they may sing thee praises
In holiness and clearness,
With consecrated lips...
O Word, eternally welling,
O aeon that never ends,
Eternal light undying,
O fount of mercy and love,
O source of all that is good!
Holy life thou art
For those who worship God!

When a heart is filled with joy, it may often overflow in song. Much of our music-making is joyous and inspired by the desire to worship, but music can express our sorrow or grief and, indeed, most other emotions as well. Anneta, the young nurse who worked in Haiti, wrote:

> There is a song I have sung many times with the refrain, "Grant us wisdom, grant us courage for the facing of this hour." Singing as a form of prayer is very real to me, and I sometimes sing out loud through those hardest times. The people in the room often join in with me, even when they are in tremendous pain.

Martin Luther said, "Next to the word of God, music describes the highest praise." And Johann Sebastian Bach wrote at the top of his manuscripts, "S.D.G." —*soli Deo Gloria*. He wanted his music to bring glory to God alone.

My grandfather once wrote that the church is "filled with such an exuberant joy of the Holy Spirit that out of the fullness of her heart she will bring praise and thanks to God, singing fervent songs overflowing with the Spirit." When we are together in a spirit of joy and worship, God will be praised in our singing.

Carolyn, a neighbor, credits parochial school with teaching her the essence of musical worship.

> I can still see Sister Benecia standing in front of our class, urging us to sing with all our hearts because, as she told us, singing is twice praying. (Later I found out that the saying is attributed to Saint Augustine.) It has stayed with me all my life, and much of my prayer life takes the form of a simple song to God.

One of the many things for which I am thankful to my parents is the love of good music they instilled in us children. We grew up listening to Bach, Beethoven, Handel, Haydn, and Mendelssohn, and learning about their lives. My parents knew that listening to classical music was also a wonderful way to learn scripture: the wonder of creation as set to music by Haydn, the story of the prophet Elijah in Mendelssohn's oratorio, the suffering and death of Christ portrayed so movingly through Bach's Passions. There is also the memorable chorus in Mendelssohn's *St. Paul:* "Oh, great is the depth of the riches of wisdom and knowledge of the Father." These works made a lasting impression on me; I remember the words to this day.

I especially love the final movement of Beethoven's *Ninth Symphony* with its words from Schiller's "Ode to Joy." For me, listening to this rousing piece is a powerful musical experience:

> You millions of people,
> Do you bend your knees before him?
> World, do you sense your creator?
> Seek him beyond the galaxies!
> He is far beyond the stars.

Nearly two hundred years after it was composed, Beethoven's glorious work continues to bring joy and hope to listeners. When the Berlin Wall came down in 1989 and a wave of freedom swept across Europe, there was no question in people's minds what music should be played to celebrate the event. While 500,000 Berliners poured across the newly opened border on Christmas Eve, conductor Leonard Bernstein led an international orchestra and choir in proclaiming the new era across the whole world with an unforgettable performance of "the Ninth." If that was not worship, what is?

18.

unity

I have lived all my life in church community. At the Bruderhof we share our earnings and hold possessions and assets in common, and in return the community cares for each person's needs, much as the early Christians did. As we share in outer things, so we also feel compelled to an inner sharing, from heart to heart. To us, such community is the essence of a truly living church. By this I mean a church in which the Holy Spirit rules, one in which there is a free and open relationship among all members, based on faith in God and trust in one another. Without this sharing of our inner lives, there is no true congregation, and thus no true community. Certainly it demands faith in God, and grace to live by this faith, but its fruits bring unparalleled blessings.

> How good and pleasant it is when brothers live together in unity! It is like precious oil poured on the head, running down on the beard, running down on Aaron's beard, down upon the collar of his robes. It is as if the dew of Hermon were falling on Mount Zion. For there the Lord bestows his blessing, even life forevermore.
>
> *Ps. 133*

Few people have the privilege of experiencing spiritual unity—our world is so torn, so divided. In our country the fabric of society has crumbled and individual lives are fragmented as never before. It is hard to imagine unity on any level. But unity can be given, and I do not mean blind conformity or similarity in outer things or uniformity, or that devilish leveling of minds called "brainwashing." Jesus said that he often wished to gather his people "as a hen gathers her chicks," and in his last prayer he pleaded that his followers be united as deeply as he is with his father. Not only that, but this unity was to be the sign by which the world would recognize his disciples.

What was so remarkable about the first Christians was their relationship to each other, their togetherness, their fellowship. This was an entirely new thing—unity. Of all the gifts of the Spirit, this was the most precious for them. They had known other kinds of fellowship before; they had known the ties of common loyalty to a group, such as a political party; they had known love of their country. But this togetherness was of a completely different order. It was not a human power at all. Those Christians literally loved one another as truly as they loved themselves.

My father-in-law, Hans, used to explain to visitors to our community that it is necessary for us to be in unity before praying together. "Prayer," he would say, "is serious business"; we are asking for real things, and therefore we have to be ready for real answers, for whatever God may ask of us.

One may well ask how unity is achieved, but in a sense that is an unanswerable question. Though we may strive for it, we will never achieve it; it is a gift just as faith is a gift. Still, a gift must be received, and if our fists are closed we are unable to take hold of it. If we keep a tight grip on our opinions, our self-image, our ambitions, we will not receive anything at all. Thus in the first place we must let go; we must remember that in our own strength we have nothing and are nothing, we must be humble and open our hearts. As members of a congregation, we should be eager to meet together, frequently and intensively, to worship God and to seek his will. Without unity, how can the church ever become more than the sum of its members, each of whom remains bound to his own values, ideals, and personal goals?

Though the prayer of a united body of believers should never replace individual prayer, it has special significance and power. It is a great gift from God when people who come from many divergent backgrounds and persuasions can be truly united. For true unity is more than emotional compatibility, more than compromise or consensus. It is the reality of being "of one heart and mind" (Acts 4:32). As my grandfather once put it:

> It is a remarkable thing when people decide something unanimously. It is the opposite of making a majority decision. Unanimity means that nobody disagrees with it or opposes it, not even in secret.
>
> We are not satisfied with finding an intellectual unanimity. It is not enough to set a common goal and use all our willpower to reach it; nor is it enough to vibrate together in an emotional experience. We know that something different has to come over us that will lift us out of this purely human level.

In the face of the hardships and difficulties (including illness, death, and other such trials) that are a part of every life at one time or another, unity is a glue that holds people together and keeps the individual from despair. A woman in my church who experienced this in a very practical way says that when unexpected illness hit her family and tested her faith like nothing before, it was the prayers of the united community around her that kept her from falling apart.

Early one morning our six-year-old daughter ran into our bedroom, saying there was blood in her bed. At first we didn't think much of it, but when it became obvious to us that this was the sort of bleeding our daughter should not be having for several more years, we grew alarmed. Earlier she had complained that her breasts were swollen and sore, and I had lined her swimsuit with soft cotton, but now this! A trip to the doctor did little to allay our fears: he told us this indicated either a brain tumor or an ovarian one.

We panicked. Our minds were whirling and our hearts were in knots. I could not keep my mind on anything, and I thought about my daughter every moment of the day. I also felt a sudden and overwhelming feeling of utter failure as a mother, how much more I should have loved her, my only daughter. We must have prayed for God's strength a hundred times in those next few days. Even though our daughter was not in pain, and our first trip or two to the hospital were uneventful, I felt like crying every time I thought of her.

Several days later, at our request, our minister told the congregation of our need. At that very instant a tremendous peace came over me. I can only explain it as a feeling of a heavy burden being lifted off my back. The church had taken it from us, and was carrying it for us. We were released from the strain of worrying for our daughter on our own and could give her over into God's care in complete trust.

During the next seven weeks multiple tests were done—
brain scans, hormone stimulation tests, and endless consul-
tations with specialists. There were some abnormal results
in the blood work, and finally a large tumor was found in
her ovary. But through it all, we were carried on wings of
peace. It almost seemed at times that perhaps we were too
unconcerned. Eventually, surgery was performed. There
was no sign of cancer; the tumor was of the type that should
have been associated with a different pattern of high hormone levels in the blood, which our daughter did not have.
The specialists were puzzled. It remained a mystery to
them; nothing made sense.

But to us it did. Hadn't our church carried this need to
God daily in hundreds of personal prayers? Hadn't a united
church interceded for her? It had, and God had heard.

19.

marriage

Within a healthy marriage, unity is evident in a unique way. Marriage is, or should be, a commitment to faithfulness for life, as many vows state, "in health and in sickness, in good times and bad, until death parts you." When two lives are shared unconditionally, there will be a full understanding of one another, a heart-to-heart relationship, an intimate sharing of all inner concerns. This leads to harmony on the deepest spiritual level, which includes the prayer life of each and of both together.

In our church communities, therefore, marriage only takes place between a man and a woman who have founded their own individual lives on God, and whose relationship to God, as far as can be discerned by the church, is firm and mature. Without this, we feel, a marriage is built on sand.

One of the questions answered by the couple at a Bruderhof wedding ceremony includes an admonition to the groom regarding the importance of respect for his bride: "...for the apostle Peter warns us that our prayers may be hindered unless we are willing to consider and honor our wives." Though it seems obvious enough that there must be a connection between the quality of a relationship with someone we love and our relationship with God, Peter's words are worth pondering more deeply, because they touch on the deepest foundation of marriage: unity of faith.

Husband and wife are more than close friends; they are bound by a mutual commitment, one they have vowed to keep sacred in two ways. One, it is exclusive, and two, it is meant to be kept forever. John asks, "How can we love God, whom we do not see, if we cannot love our brother, whom we do see?" In light of this question, the parallel between a good marriage and a fruitful prayer life is plain. If I lack the compassion, honesty, and humility to honor the person I am closest to in this world – the love of my life – it is hardly plausible that I will have it in me to commune fruitfully with God through prayer.

There is yet another dimension to prayer in a marriage: its stabilizing effect in helping overcome differences between the two partners, no matter how incompatible their personalities might seem, if they are determined to stay together. The following words of Jack and Jean, a couple in my congregation, amply illustrate this:

> We both have the strong tendency of wanting our own way and are all too ready to defend our own point of view. In our marriage of twenty-eight years, it happened much too often that we would get into a deadlock situation. We have had to deal with our differences and arguments, and it has been painful. We had to work hard to keep our marriage together.
>
> It was prayer that helped us to break the cycle of hurting each other with a sarcastic remark or criticism. By praying together daily, we have found it possible to get beyond "just the two of us," beyond hurt feelings and pride. It takes humility and honesty. It takes knowing you need it, but that's not enough. We have to *ask* for it, in prayer. But

it means praying for it together; it has to be the longing of both of us. We have found that any unresolved grudge toward the other kills our prayer. But when we are united, prayer provides a certainty to keep at it, to keep going.

Clergy and parents of young people need to ask: do we give sufficient guidance and help to couples considering marriage? Young adults in love should be made aware of the danger of admiring each other solely (even primarily) because of physical or sexual attractiveness; if this dominates a relationship, it will surely go sour. For a relationship to last, both partners must seek and find what is of God in the other.

Dale, a friend over many years, wrote the letter below to a couple in my church at the time of their wedding. It captures the spiritual basis for marriage concisely and deeply.

We are with you in mind and heart and spirit on this day of your coming together before God as a unity for life. We wish you every happiness – knowing full well that most happiness comes only with work and struggle.

So, in effect, we are wishing you much work and much struggle. But let it be said, the paradox is that therein lies the blessing.

No one ever learned anything of value riding the crest of success. But sooner or later every wave breaks – it all comes down. It's guaranteed: whatever wave we are surfing on will break. And we find ourselves in the deep, treading water while tons more pours down on us.

This is when the swimming becomes hard. Gasping for air, desperate to survive but with no means to do so, this is where the empty, open hand that has no option but faith finds the hand of God. Now learning begins. It is terrifying. And it is a gift.

One of the many blessings of a marriage based in the Holy Spirit and Jesus Christ is that two seekers can thrust their hands up together, that like Aaron holding up Moses' arms, two can support each other when the strength of one is not enough.

But there is a danger in that too—we must be clear that two people with little strength are barely more powerful than one person with little strength. The most we can do for each other is hold up the arms to God—only God's power will overcome.

This is my prayer for you—that no matter how tired you are, how frustrated, how discouraged, how fed up, how angry, how disappointed or disillusioned—no matter—that in spite of it you will always rush to the side of the other to hold up your spouse's arms in prayer lest the other become too tired to pray, too tired to reach up one more time and find the hand of God. And just like Moses and Aaron, you will always see that God is faithful to his promises, that as you hold each other up in prayer, two as one, the spiritual battle will turn to the side of the light.

You never know what will happen in a marriage; it is usually what you are least prepared for. My parents were married for over forty years, and for many of those years my father was a very sick man. He was often close to death. We were sure he would die before my mother. She was the healthy and active one, swimming, hiking, and working in the garden for hours. Then, all of a sudden, like a lightning bolt out of the blue, my mother was found to have cancer. She died only five months after the diagnosis.

Aside from serious illness, married couples will go through plenty of experiences that require a foundation of unshakeable unity in the facing of difficulties. A partner may suffer an emotional breakdown. Or the woman may have a miscarriage. Or perhaps the couple is infertile and cannot have children. They may lose a child through death. Will they stand by each other in support and in prayer? Is their bond strong enough to weather any crisis?

As children grow up, there will be plenty of tensions between the parents. A cute three-year-old turns into a mischievous schoolboy who needs loving guidance, and in the turbulent years of adolescence, the innocent child becomes a sulky, rebellious teenager.

If prayer is ever needed, it is in a marriage; there has to be daily prayer and daily forgiveness. A young husband in my church wrote to me:

> Taking time to pray together in the morning and at night before bed is a very powerful thing that I appreciate more and more each day. The morning used to be the hardest for me, but I have come to realize what an effect it has to take this time to turn to the Lord, even if in just a few words. At night, following prayer, we both sleep better. After our morning prayer I can feel this peace being given to my wife, as I also experience it myself. It is amazing what a difference this makes for the rest of the day. I firmly believe that prayer is vital for a marriage. I would even say it is the duty of a husband and wife to take the time to pray together and for each other.

The celibate life can be an unbearable burden for the person who does not feel it to be his or her personal calling. Nevertheless, through actively seeking God's will, peace of heart can be found. The answer is in unity, not with another person in the most intimate sense, but with fellow believers in the unity of the church, and ultimately, unity with God. If such a person does not succumb to the bitterness that results from frustrated desire, but instead overcomes its magnetic power, he or she can live purely and fully in God's love. Fara, the daughter of close friends, writes:

> I am forty-five years old and single, and I'll admit I didn't feel the calling to celibacy.
>
> As a young woman I had all the natural feelings of longing and dreams for a partner. In fact, I often thought I was in love with one or the other young man. But every time it turned out to be only from my side.
>
> One by one my friends married, and each time I struggled with jealousy and self-pity. Why was I not given this gift? What was wrong with me? How could I bear to stay single—never to have a husband, never to have children?
>
> In my need, I turned to my minister, not once but many times. He directed me to turn to God in prayer, which opened my eyes and heart to something much greater: the fact that by the very sacrifice of marriage, I could do something for God *and* I could do it in joy. I did not have to circle around my singleness. This was not a onetime realization. Over and over I had to pray for acceptance.
>
> Repeatedly I have fallen short of this calling, but I believe it is possible with the help of God. And I have been able to find joy in giving up marriage for the sake of God. Even now, after so many years, I have moments or hours of longing or loneliness, but as time goes by, this question has become of less and less importance to me. For many years I have had the privilege and joy of working with children, and I have had the chance to serve others in ways that I couldn't have, had I been married.

I believe that one can live a totally fulfilled life as a single person, even if one has not felt the calling to celibacy. Christ can fill every void.

Although a meaningful sphere of human experience is closed to the unmarried, of all people it is they who can be granted a rich fulfillment and happiness in life, in service to others and to God. In fact, every one of us needs to be fully redeemed in this area, for a marriage partner must never become more important than God, and marriage should never be a distraction from our personal relationship with him.

I have known Roger and Lillian since my childhood. They met and were married in our church but went through long, hard struggles and lived separately for years. Their story is a wonderful example of what can be given through prayer. Lillian writes:

> I owe the foundation of my faith to the school I went to from ten to eighteen. We had assembly every morning – we called it Prayers. We sang a psalm and a hymn. That is when I learned many psalms by heart, and they meant a great deal to me. We said the Lord's Prayer together, but as this was done every day, it became a habit. Still, through those years a firm trust in God and belief in Jesus grew in my heart.
>
> I left school when I was eighteen. On the last morning at Prayers, the headmistress read Psalm 91, especially for the graduating class. She said, "Take it with you through life." I have turned to it again and again in times of struggle.

During her university years, Lillian attended a church where there was a lively youth group. Through the sermons and discussions they began to think seriously about discipleship: what does it mean to *believe* the words of Jesus, and to act on them? Soon they were involved in social work, trying to help the poor in various ways, though realizing that even the best efforts did little to change the gross injustices inherent in the "system."

It was then that Lillian met my uncle, Hardy, who was studying in England, and talked to him about her frustration. He said, "You cannot change the system or the ways of the world. You can only change yourself."

Hardy's words made a strong impression on Lillian and others in her church. As she later recognized, they also contained a vital key to winning the longest battle of her life: struggling to remain loyal and loving to the man she married.

> In June 1937, Roger and I were married. But our marriage went through one conflict and crisis after another on account of his homosexuality. The church was a great support to me in those times when he was away for long periods. When distressing letters came from him, I got discouraged and sometimes gave up praying for him. But I always came back to it, as it was the only thing I could do to help him. I knew that everything is possible with God, and that someday my husband might be restored to me and to the church.
>
> I can never cease to feel what a miracle it was when Roger came back in his old age. I loved being with him; he was so different. He was humble and simple in his thinking. He loved those around him very deeply, and they loved him. He was very close to God, especially in the last months before his death at the age of ninety-one. I think of him every day and will always treasure the time I had with him.

I think he was closer to the kingdom than I am. Too late I think of things I could have done, see where I failed in love. But God is faithful and keeps his promises.

20.

unanswered
prayer

Amy Carmichael grew up in Ireland in the late 1800s and went to India as a missionary. Adopting that country as her home, she never returned to Ireland but devoted the rest of her life to rescuing children from temple prostitution. With a handful of Indian women, she saved hundreds of female babies from their certain fate—a life of sexual slavery at the hands of Hindu priests—and raised them communally in Dohnavur, a settlement she founded for this purpose.

Amy loved her mother's bright blue eyes, and as a little girl she was not happy with her own brown ones. So she decided to pray for blue eyes, and in her childlike trust was perfectly convinced that God would answer her prayer the way she hoped. But it did not happen:

> Without a shadow of a doubt that my eyes would be blue in the morning, I had gone to sleep, and the minute I woke I went to the looking-glass, full of eager expectation, and saw—brown eyes. I don't remember how the words came, "Isn't *no* an answer?" Perhaps my mother, whose blue eyes had made me so much want to change my brown ones, said something of the sort.

Much later in her life, among the brown-eyed women of India, she realized the gift God had given her. Blue eyes would have marked her immediately as a foreigner and blocked her way to the hearts of many people.

For most of us, of course, the issue of "unanswered" prayer has little to do with such a childlike wish. The things we pray for as adults are pressing needs – or so we think. As I see it, the primary question is whether we are ready to accept God's leading in our lives. Is our attitude really "thy will be done"? In a sense, we should not even worry whether God answers our petitions or not, but ought to be comforted by the fact that he knows our needs and has heard our request. He may not answer us the way we want, but perhaps in a much better and more wonderful way.

In the Bible our relationship with God is often compared to that of a father with his children. Like a parent, God can give us one of three answers, the same ones we give our own children: yes, no, or not now. As parents, we don't always say yes. Just as frequently we say no, or not now. Why should God treat us any differently?

Deborah, a childhood acquaintance who is now a grandmother, recently reflected on the many occasions in her life when God answered her prayers in unexpected ways, as in this instance:

> Sometimes we are slow to see that our prayer has been answered, because the answer is not what we expect. All four of our children were born after I was thirty-six, and each time the doctors told me that there was a high risk of having a handicapped child. Our first three were normal, healthy children, but before our fourth was born, there were several signs that not all was well. When Joanna arrived,

I was relieved to see how beautiful she was, but knew she was very weak and obviously not normal. We had prayed for her through my entire pregnancy, and we continued to do so even after her birth, hoping for a miracle. But Joanna did not get stronger and healthier. She was found to have Prader-Willi Syndrome, a rare condition in which the child is mentally hindered in most areas – though often quite advanced in language skills – and prone to behavioral difficulties, such as an insatiable appetite, which generally leads to morbid obesity. Joanna's diagnosis was hard enough to accept as it was, but then a nurse made it even worse. She said, "You would have been better off with a Down child."

I was rebellious, full of questions. Why me? What have I done to deserve this? And in spite of loving her, there were moments when I felt she was a burden on our family. Only slowly has it dawned on me that Joanna is less a burden than a gift, especially in her way of helping me learn about patience and love. It is not by scales falling from my eyes, not through just one incident, that I have come to this acceptance of Joanna. The process has been slow and sometimes painful. We are told that love is patient and kind – and I am neither. But Joanna is. Maybe the answer to my many prayers is this: even if God did not change my child, he has changed me.

Genuine prayer is an opening of the heart and mind for God's will to be done in our lives. As Martin Luther King Jr. put it: "The idea that man expects God to do everything leads inevitably to a callous misuse of prayer. For if God does everything, man then asks him for anything, and God becomes little more than a 'cosmic bellhop' who is summoned for every trivial need."

In striving for greater humility, it is always fruitful to examine our personal lives for whatever obstacles might be preventing God's will from becoming reality in our lives. But to do this we must really believe that he is a better judge of what we need, because he knows us better than we know ourselves. That is the essence of trust: not only hoping, but *knowing* that God will find the best answers for us.

> I asked for power that I might achieve;
>> He made me meek that I might obey.
> I asked for health that I might do greater things;
>> I was given grace that I might do better things.
> I asked for riches that I might be happy;
>> I was given poverty that I might be wise.
> I asked for strength that I might have the praise of men;
>> I was given weakness that I might feel the need of God.
> I asked for all things that I might enjoy life;
>> I was given life that I might enjoy all things.
> I received nothing that I asked for, but all that I hoped for;
>> My prayer was answered.
>
> *Anonymous*

Sometimes it seems that God creates certain circumstances in a person's life so that he can use us for his purposes. But then we have to be willing to be used. Like Fara in the previous chapter, Connie is a single woman whose prayers were not answered in the way she had hoped.

> I prayed many times for marriage because of the words in the gospel: ask for whatever you want, and it will be given. I firmly believed that God would give me marriage, and many times I felt sure that he had heard me. Later, however, I would feel let down because nothing happened.
>
> It has taken me years (perhaps I am spiritually dull) but I have finally discovered that when I forgot all about my

hopes for a husband and reached out to others, my emptiness was overcome.

No prayer goes up to heaven that is not heard and answered.
We may not always see the answer—it may not be obvious,
or we may have missed it because we were looking else-
where—but that does not mean it isn't there.

> What happens to all those prayers when not only are they
> not "answered," but things get far worse than anyone ever
> anticipated? Surely the prayers have sustained me, are sus-
> taining me. Perhaps there will be unexpected answers to
> these prayers, answers I may not even be aware of for years.
> But they are not wasted. They are not lost. I do not know
> where they have gone, but I believe God holds them, hand
> outstretched to receive them like precious pearls.
>
> *Madeleine L'Engle*

Without going into the age-old question of why an
almighty God allows his children to go through pain and
suffering, I venture to say that such times can bring us
closer to him. Through suffering, either our own or that of
someone we love, we can experience God, but it depends
entirely on whether we are inwardly receptive to what he
wants to give us. Because we tend to pray most intensely in
times of sickness or impending death—for an illness to be
cured, or a life saved—the disappointment or frustration we
sense when we feel our prayers are not answered is intensified too. Many religious writers tell us the reason prayers
are not answered is our lack of faith, and this may be so.
Yet the Bible tells us that death is the last enemy, a clear
reminder that until the kingdom comes on earth—until our
world is completely won for God—the course of our lives

simply will remain subject to powers of death and darkness, no matter how faithful we are.

Christa, a mother of two, has grappled with this reality ever since her husband abandoned her:

> I have sometimes wondered how we should pray when, humanly seen, the answer to our prayers looks all but impossible. It seems that, if we are always praying for a certain outcome, such as the return of a loved one or a miraculous cure for cancer, we only set ourselves up for disappointment. But if we simply pray for God's will to be done, and trust that he loves us, we can be at peace and know that the right thing will happen. And we should remember what is of eternal value. In my case this may mean that, even more than praying for my husband to return, I pray that God has mercy on his soul and brings him to repentance.

The Gospel of Luke records the words of Jesus: "Ask, and it will be given to you; seek, and you will find; knock, and the door will be opened to you. For every one who asks receives, and he who seeks finds, and to him who knocks the door will be opened." God always opens doors, even if they are not the ones we would have chosen. At the same time we should not forget the wonderful words of Scripture: "For what father among you, if his son asks for a fish, will give him a serpent, or if he asks for an egg, will give him a scorpion? If you then who are evil, know how to give good gifts to your children, how much more will the heavenly Father give the Holy Spirit to those who ask him!" What tremendous words – and what an encouragement for those times when we feel God has not heard us.

The Gospel of Matthew records similar words of Jesus: "Seek first the kingdom of God and its righteousness, and then all other things will be given to you." About this promise C.S. Lewis writes: "Infinite comfort in the second part; inexorable demand in the first. Hopeless if it were to be done by your own endeavors...God must do it."

This is an invaluable inner direction for our prayer life, for we focus too easily on our personal desires, and our prayer requests are insignificant when we see them in the light of God's kingdom. Kierkegaard writes, "Prayer does not change God. It changes him who prays." All the more then, we ought to remember the importance of the still small voice, the value of inner quiet, and the necessity of a listening heart. For without these, he cannot change us.

21.

miracles

When Jesus sent out his disciples, he gave them the power and authority to perform miracles. Demons were driven out, the sick were healed, and the dead were raised. Today, many people, even among Christians, find these stories fantastic and either dismiss them outright or explain them away. All the same I believe that miracles are real, and that they play a greater part in our lives than we recognize. And further, I believe we do not sufficiently acknowledge God's intervention in our lives. Even when we do, the passage of time often causes us to forget how wonderfully God has answered our prayers, and we are left remembering only those times when we felt disappointed.

Earlier in this book I mentioned Johann Christoph Blumhardt, a nineteenth-century pastor through whom many were led to God. After he died in 1880, his son Christoph Friedrich carried on his father's work until his own death in 1919. Despite their obvious apostolic powers, neither father nor son were pious in a conventional way. If anything, they were straightforward and down-to-earth to the point of being blunt. Christoph Friedrich once wrote:

> We can kill Christ with our Christianity! After all, what is more important – Christianity or Christ? Yes, we can even kill Christ with our prayers. When we approach God full of

self-importance, our prayers are useless. Many people pray only for their own honor and satisfaction and don't think of the kingdom of God or of the glory of God. When any comfort is lacking they complain and cry, "O dear Father in heaven, bless us! Protect our investments!" Thus they cry and weep, and with their prayers they kill Christ.

In 1842 the elder Blumhardt found himself and his family faced with a woman in great emotional and spiritual distress. Gottliebin Dittus, a member of Blumhardt's parish in Möttlingen, had often been ill, and walking was difficult for her, as one leg was shorter than the other.

Magical practices and superstitious beliefs were rampant in the village at the time, and Gottliebin was no stranger to them. From childhood on, she had had uncanny experiences, and had gradually become involved in the occult. Now, at twenty-seven, she uttered strange sounds and used different voices. Repeatedly she saw a woman holding a dead child. There were banging noises in her house at night, and she began to have spells of unconsciousness. Once she was found in a pool of blood, and another time she tried to hang herself.

After two years of torment, Gottliebin came to Blumhardt and confessed various sins in the hope that it would help her. But there was no relief. Soon crowds began to gather at the Dittus house to witness the supernatural occurrences. Though fully aware of the dangers inherent in attempting to confront evil spirits, Blumhardt reluctantly decided to step in. Strangely, Gottliebin, when faced with this man of God, could not bear to look at him or hear his prayers.

One day, as she lay unconscious on the floor, Blumhardt announced in a loud, commanding voice: "We have seen enough of what the devil can do. Now let us see what God can do!" At this, to the astonishment of those present, Gottliebin awoke and prayed with him. Thus began a long and intense struggle against the darkness that was binding the woman's soul. Gottliebin continued to suffer under the attacks; in fact, they grew progressively more violent. Before long, her sister Katharina began to suffer similarly. As those around the women prayed for their souls, they experienced the tumult and drama of two spirit worlds clashing head-on. For his part, Blumhardt refused to yield from his firm belief that prayer was the one and only weapon strong enough to overcome the powers of darkness. He was proved right: after two grueling years, the battle ended in complete victory and peace.

It was very early one morning – two o'clock – when Katharina, gripped by one final contortion, cried out, "Jesus is the victor!" Blumhardt wrote, "The strength and power of the demon now appeared to wane with every passing minute, growing more and more quiet, moving less and less, finally leaving her body altogether – but not until eight in the morning – just as the light of life might go out of a dying person. At this point the fight came to an end. True, there still remained various things to deal with afterwards, but it was merely like clearing away the rubble of a collapsed building." The two women, completely freed from their torments, joined the Blumhardt's household; Gottliebin even remained with him the rest of her days, working, praying, and counseling the many needy souls drawn there by the hope her victory gave them.

Through the miracle of healing a movement of repentance began in Blumhardt's parish. Hundreds of people – even complete strangers – came to him to confess their sins. Mental and emotional burdens were lifted and the sick were healed.

Not that the pastor would have anything to do with sorcery or even curiosity about it – to him, the remedy for spiritual darkness was not an understanding of it, but prayer. Indeed, prayer was the essence of Blumhardt's ministry. "The people seeking my help are burdened souls who do not find comfort or the strength, either from within or from without, to free themselves…The only thing I do is to awaken their trust in God and lead them to confident prayer to him."

From all over Germany, and even from Holland and Switzerland, people flocked to Blumhardt's parish. Soon he had to find a larger place. He purchased a former spa and developed it into a sort of spiritual retreat center. The miracles given by God in those years were so powerful that when my wife and I traveled there in the 1960s and 1970s, we could still sense something of them. Though difficult to describe, the spirit we felt might best be summed up as an awareness of God's greatness, and the smallness of our lives in the face of eternity. A carved plaque on the wall of Gottliebin's house, placed there over a century ago, captures this well. Translated from the German, it reads:

O man, think on eternity;
mock not the time still given thee,
for judgment cometh speedily.

After his father's death the younger Blumhardt increasingly tried to deflect attention from the healing power of prayer because he felt that too much emphasis was being placed on the experiences of particular individuals. "It would be better for people to remain sick than to go around chattering about their healing." He lamented the lack of reverence for what God had done, and feared that his house would be seen as an institution for faith healing. As he wrote in a letter:

There is a dishonesty that exploits the mercy and grace of God in such a way that the Savior becomes our servant, who is merely expected to restore again and again what we have spoiled. A selfish streak has crept in among us. This pains my heart, and I have decided to find a new attitude toward those who come to me in need and affliction. It is God's honor we must exalt in our own persons, both physically and spiritually. Not our own well-being must be in the foreground, but only God...Leave for a time your begging before God, and do not look at your own suffering; turn your inner being in the opposite direction, and look at the suffering of God, whose kingdom has been held up for so long.

For the Blumhardts, healing, even of dire ailments, was significant only insofar as it furthered the coming of the kingdom of God on earth. Unless God is present in our hearts—unless his justice is manifest in our daily lives—our physical well-being is insignificant. More than anything else, they felt, suffering souls need to be pointed to the three great supplications in the Lord's Prayer: thy name be honored, thy kingdom come, thy will be done.

Sundar Singh was born in 1889 to a wealthy Sikh family in India. There was nothing he lacked—money, food, fine clothing, luxury and abundance of every kind. At fifteen, Sundar Singh had a vision of Jesus and experienced a conversion. Immediately, he was persecuted by his family, who said they would sooner see him dead than a Christian. Once, he was given poisoned food and became so ill the doctors considered his survival a miracle. Sundar Singh was baptized by Western missionaries, but soon left them to follow the footsteps of Christ in a manner more suited to his background: he became a wandering holy man, or sadhu.

Sundar Singh traveled throughout Asia and Europe and twice went to England and America, where he was distressed by the excess of materialism on the one hand and the absence of prayer on the other. Everywhere he made a profound impression on those who met him. My grandfather heard Sundar Singh speak in 1922 and was so impressed by him that he gave every member of his congregation a copy of Sundar Singh's biography. Here was a man of rare conviction, a man for whom discipleship meant following one's beliefs no matter what the cost.

Numerous times Sundar Singh experienced divine protection. In one of the most striking incidents, in Tibet (where missionaries were not permitted), he was captured after preaching, tried, and thrown into a dry well whose lid was then closed and locked. As he fell, his right arm was badly injured, but he survived and spent the next three days in darkness without food or water. On the third night, just as Sundar Singh was crying to God in prayer, he heard a grating sound: someone was opening the locked lid of the well. A rope was thrown down, and he was gently pulled up. Then the lid was closed again, and locked. Sundar Singh turned to thank his deliverer, but there was no one to be seen.

He was free, and even the pain in his arm was gone. Undeterred, he went back to the same town and took up his preaching once more. Again he was arrested and taken before a judge, the same one who had ordered him thrown in the well. Amazed, the man inquired who had freed Sundar Singh, but no one could tell him. There was only one key to the lid of the well, and it was still hanging from the judge's

own girdle. The sadhu was ordered to leave the city immediately, lest his powerful God bring disaster upon the people.

With regard to the miracles he experienced, Sundar Singh
said nothing to deny or defend them. He frequently insisted
that there was "no power in these hands," claiming that
the only miracle is the power of God in answer to prayer.
When asked whether he had ever tried spiritual healing, he
answered, "Yes, but I gave it up because I found it made
people look to me and not to God, and that is a cross I cannot bear."

Another time he was asked, "How much of your prayer is
petition, and how much of it is communion?" "For the first
two or three years after my conversion," he replied, "I used
to ask for specific things. Now I ask for God."

Several chapters back I wrote about the difficulties our
community experienced under Hitler, hardships that pale in
comparison with the suffering of the Jews and millions of
others, yet still altered the course of our history.

Many amazing things happened during those years, and
although some events may appear coincidental, there is little
doubt in my mind that they were an answer to prayer. Someone once said, "Coincidence is a pseudonym God uses when
he prefers not to sign his name." Only once, for instance, in
all our years in Germany, did we have visitors from North
America, and they came just during the week that the community was surrounded and raided by the Nazis.

On April 14, 1937, secret police descended on the Bruderhof, and all men, women, and children were ordered to
gather in the dining hall to hear a proclamation. Our own
people were of course apprehensive, but our visitors from

America were not. One of them, who spoke German, grabbed the commander by his lapel: "Watch what you are doing. We will tell all America what we see here."

Once assembled, all Bruderhof members were ordered to disperse within the next twenty-four hours, either returning to relatives or to their hometowns. Later that day the order was modified: the Nazis agreed to allow them to leave the country in groups and find refuge in England and Liechtenstein. Who knows what might have happened but for the presence of two American visitors, who recorded everything they saw?

The following day, three members—Hans, Hannes, and Karl—were ordered to get into a Gestapo car and were taken away. By afternoon it was clear that they were not coming back. As their wives and families later found out, the three had been driven to the Nazi district headquarters, taken into "protective custody," and locked in a cell. Hours became days, and days turned into weeks. One day Karl was informed that despite his objections, he was going to be inducted into military service as he was German (the other two men were Swiss). All three of them declared that they would not submit under any circumstance, and wrote a joint statement addressed to the highest local official. The following day Karl was taken from his cell. While he was gone, Hannes and Hans went on their knees and remained there, pleading that Karl be protected and given strength. Miraculously, he was brought back unharmed within hours.

A few days later, the three men were suddenly ordered to gather their belongings and follow a guard to the iron gates outside the prison, where a black car stood waiting for them. Certain that they were headed for concentration camp, the men refused to get in. At this they were handed a letter from their lawyer, instructing them to go with the driver of the car and head for Holland. Perplexed but relieved, they jumped in, and the driver took off at high speed. An hour later he stopped in the middle of a forest, glanced around to make sure no one was watching, motioned them to get out, and pointed in the direction of the Dutch border. With that he sped off and was gone, never to be heard of again.

Crossing into Holland through a forest in the middle of the night was a risky undertaking. When the brothers lost their way and came out on the German side, a guard stopped them. Incredibly, they were able to convince him that friends on the other side of the border expected them, and he not only let them across but also showed them the way to the nearest Dutch village. From there they made their way to England. Years later, Karl chuckled over the incident:

> We were creeping quietly through the woods for a very long time. Hannes was walking in front, and suddenly he started singing! I thought he was crazy, but he said he was sure we were safely over the border, so I started singing too. We walked on, singing at the top of our lungs. Suddenly a loud voice said, *"Halt!"* My heart sank. It was a border guard, who questioned us and looked at our papers but then let us go. We must have seemed like fools, walking through the woods in the middle of the night, singing. As for our papers—I can only think an angel must have held a hand over the guard's eyes: none of our passports were valid!

God intervenes in our lives at many points and in many different ways. During the first arduous years of the Bruderhof, a time of dire poverty, our members experienced this intervention repeatedly, through friends and strangers, and through unexpected gifts of money.

In the summer of 1922, our community became embroiled in tensions. Though the community's basis of faith was a hallmark of its founding, several members had begun to criticize it as financially unwise. As the crisis came to a head, there were some major payments due, but, as usual, no money. My grandparents, away on a mission journey, set off to return, trusting that God would intervene; they mentioned their need to no one. Just before they left, they were approached by Maria Mojen, an acquaintance whose father was an Indonesian prince. She handed them an envelope, "for the cause." In it was sufficient money to repay all the outstanding bank loans.

In 1926 the community moved to an old farm in the Rhön mountains, several miles away from its first location. The place was rundown but had a favorable asking price: 26,000 marks. No one knew where the 10,000 marks required for the down payment would come from, nor how they would ever be able to finance the repair of the houses. Nevertheless, they decided to take a step in faith and buy the place. Ten days before the money was due, there were still no funds, yet the members held firm in their belief that God would show them a way if it was to happen. Then, the last day before the down payment was due, a local nobleman, the Prince of Schönburg-Waldenburg, sent 10,000 marks. As my grandmother wrote in her memoirs, "Our jubilation knew no bounds! Everyone gathered in the house, and we sang one song of praise and thanksgiving after another."

Finances were constantly tight at the Bruderhof in those years, and in 1928, when the community seemed in danger once again of defaulting on several large loans, the courts decided to auction the entire property. Again, disaster was averted at the last moment by the unexpected gift of 5000 Swiss francs from a friend.

After the Nazis seized power in 1933, government regulations became more and more repressive, and week by week there were new developments for the community to contend with. By the end of the year, the Bruderhof school was closed: the children were to be sent to a public school. At that juncture, the community whisked all its school-age children, including the orphans and foster children in its care, across the border to Switzerland, where they and two young women, their teachers, found temporary lodging in a vacant children's home.

By spring long-term housing in the form of a spartan but roomy summer hotel high in the Liechtenstein Alps was located but, as usual, there was no money to buy or rent it. Around the same time a twenty-year mortgage payment was suddenly demanded with only two weeks' notice, the community's permit to sell books and other merchandise was revoked, and all government support was withdrawn. On top of this the children's home in Switzerland announced that it could not extend its hospitality any further—not even for one more week. Just during these days, my grandparents visited Julia, a guest at the Bruderhof the previous summer, who was hospitalized with back trouble. As they left, Julia pressed into their hands the sum of 6500 Swiss francs, enough money for the first installment on the summer hotel.

One could go on for many pages with stories of timely help when things looked hopeless. Each time, it seemed, God intervened in answer to prayer—or simply in answer to our need.

Few of us experience great personal miracles in our life-times; answers to small prayers are more usual. Yet many people do not even believe that God responds to prayer. Retired Archbishop Alex Brunett of Seattle, an acquaintance, feels that no matter what skeptics say, it has power to change lives and outcomes.

> I remember when I was a chaplain at Eastern Michigan University in Ypsilanti, and there was a serial killer going around raping young women and killing them. The atmosphere at the college was very, very tense. People were afraid. When was this man going to strike again? And people turned to prayer. And the intensity of prayer became so powerful that they felt sure the man would be found, and why? — because the whole place was filled with prayer.
>
> Within a week's time he was arrested. That was only one of many times in my life when I felt that prayer moves mountains.

Anna Mow, a missionary in India in the 1920s and 30s, and later a professor at Chicago's Bethany Seminary, was a close friend over many decades. She had a wonderful sense of humor and an inimitable cackle, and everywhere she moved she took her favorite painting: a picture of Jesus laughing. During her long life she experienced countless incidents of answered prayer, but this never seemed to surprise her. To her, it was the natural consequence of turning to God.

At ninety-one, Anna suffered a stroke that left her partially paralyzed, and though her faith and humor were not affected, her speech was. Jane, a speech therapist, offered a regimen of exercises, but Anna felt insulted and would not cooperate. Finally, Jane was advised by Anna's family simply to converse with her. If she shared a burden or need with Anna, they said, she would surely feel stimulated and respond in some way. Over the next several sessions of therapy, a warm friendship developed between them; they talked about life, about God, and about faith. Jane even revealed the greatest sorrow of her life: for years she and her husband had wanted a child, but despite the best help she had been unable to conceive. A few months later, Anna died. Her involvement in Jane's life was not over, however. At the funeral, Jane whispered to one of Anna's granddaughters, "I'm pregnant!"

Unexpected outcomes from illness or medical conditions may not be rare, but the person who believes in God will often sense his love at work. Skeptics claim that such things "just happen" now and then, that it has nothing to do with God or miracles or prayer. Nonetheless, such happenings remain humanly inexplicable. And what is a miracle, if not an unexpected outcome in which we see the hand of God?

22.

prayer in
daily life

In my book *Why Forgive?* I wrote about Gordon Wilson and his daughter Marie, who was killed by a bomb in Enniskillen, Northern Ireland. Gordon died recently, but his widow Joan is carrying on their work for peace. She writes:

> The day of the bombing we waited and watched and prayed. At first I was very angry. I felt, how could anyone do such a thing? And then I thought of the Lord's Prayer how we ask, "Forgive us our trespasses as we forgive those who trespass against us" – and of Jesus' words, "Father, forgive them, for they know not what they do." These words kept ringing through my mind regarding the men who set the bomb; I felt they just didn't *know* what they were doing. People would say, Oh, yes, they do, they just don't care, and one day they are going to have to face their Judge, and it's going to catch up with them. But I prayed that they would realize what they had done, and that they would ask for forgiveness. It took me a long time to sort this out and live with it. I still go over it in my mind every day – the bomb, my daughter's death, forgiveness, prayer. I hate what they did, but I don't hate them.
>
> Before the bomb I was sometimes very flippant about Good Friday. I remember saying, "I really don't understand

Easter very well." But after Marie died, I prayed. I remember grieving very deeply one day and wondering, "Is there no one who can help me?" Suddenly a voice seemed to say, "I am a man of sorrows and acquainted with grief." And then it came to me: on the cross, Jesus went through every sorrow there is. He is the only one who can help me and bring me through. I also realized that what I went through was nothing, absolutely nothing, compared to what Jesus suffered.

One can pray in many different places and in different ways. Sometimes prayer doesn't come easily; at other times it flows. Prayer can be silence, singing, reading, even walking, for we can talk to God anywhere.

For me prayer is a daily pattern, a daily discipline. I've reached a stage where I feel I must pray about everything. Yet prayer is not a duty, it's a privilege. It's a blessing to talk to God and to know that he will hear and answer. I pray for my neighbors and loved ones, for people who come to my house, for the sick, and of course for the political situation. There is the whole world to pray for! I could spend all day on my knees. But I can also talk to God as I go about my daily tasks. That is the great thing.

In Thessalonians 5, Paul gives us three wonderful commandments: to rejoice, to pray without ceasing, and to give thanks in all things. In a sense, these three are all one, for to a person who has a living relationship with God, all three – rejoicing, praying, and giving thanks – will be as much a part of life as eating and drinking. Kierkegaard once said, "Why do I breathe? Because otherwise I would die – and so it is with praying." To me, Kierkegaard's answer is the simplest and best reply to the age-old question, "How can I pray without ceasing?" In his eyes, a life lived in relation to the Eternal is one endless prayer.

Carolyn, a neighbor of mine whose thoughts on worship I quoted earlier, says:

> For me, prayer is a running conversation with God, whom I address as Dear Father. Prayer for me is something very natural, and yet it is also an act of the will. By an act of the will I mean that sometimes, when I open my eyes in the morning, I know the first thing I want to do is to thank God for the new day and ask for his protection over my loved ones. At other times, though, I am grumpy and don't feel like talking to him, but I do it anyway.
>
> Of course it is always easier to pray in times of trouble. When I was a troubled teenager struggling for a direction in my life, I sat on the beach and talked to God and felt he was close to me—that he would help me and protect me. It gave me a new determination to give value to my life.
>
> Now I'm over fifty, and I look back and feel somewhat ashamed. I think about the many holy people who pray and meditate. Somehow that's just not where I am at. I ask myself, have I really given myself enough in prayer to God? Surely not, but I ask God to have mercy on me.
>
> I can't imagine life without some kind of talking things over with God. Sometimes, when I have made a real fool of myself, I talk to God and try to see it from his perspective—that I really am a foolish person. I try to laugh at myself. Or, during times of need, for instance when my husband had a heart attack or when I had a miscarriage, we prayed a lot. We didn't use big words, but just turned our lives over to God and asked for his will to be done. Many things in our lives have not been easy or turned out the way we might have wanted them, but if any one prayer has been consistent in our lives, it has been the prayer for God's will to be done.

In the rush of life, there is always something that has to be done, something to distract us from what is really important. Part of the answer is to prioritize the many things that come to our attention. Often prayer is the first thing we neglect—perhaps because we feel it demands space or time or privacy. Yet why should this be so? If our relationship to God is alive, we will always feel that the channels to him are open, so to speak, and we will lift our thoughts to him regularly, no matter the outward circumstances.

Still, Cardinal Donald Wuerl of Washington points out that it is a good practice to put aside time just for prayer:

> You have to make that time, in order to hear God speaking to you, and you need time to respond back to him. There is no way that a relationship can be built in silence, in the sense of noncommunication. Amid the clatter of life, we have to find the silence of recollection, the centeredness in our lives to allow us to hear God. Then the gifts of the Spirit are revealed: peace, joy, love, and faith.

Reggie, a prison inmate in Pennsylvania, knows how true this is. He writes:

> At the low-slung steel and stone prison fortress where I live, a permanent darkness hangs over everything. The desecration of life is everywhere, even in the constant stream of talk that fills the air: gossip and profanity, anger and anguished wails, malicious backbiting and smutty jokes. But because I have made a covenant with Allah, the one true God, to perform the five canonical prayers of the Muslim faith every day, no amount of darkness can overpower me.
>
> To me, *salah* (obligatory prayer) is an act of ablution that removes the filthy stains of Satan by means of self-purification. In an environment of corruption and dirt and death, prayer cleanses the temple of my spirit. In prayer I bow my

mind and heart to the will of Allah in *taqwa* (purity, piety, righteousness, and fear of Allah) and promise to remember him as he remembers me.

In our age of cynicism and superficiality, ever smaller numbers believe that God hears our prayers when we turn to him. Even when people do pray and their requests are granted, they may shrug it off as a happy coincidence that has nothing to do with God.

Watching TV one evening the following words from the Quran (S. 6:63) leapt to mind:

> Say, who is it that delivereth
> you from the dark recesses
> of land and sea,
> when ye call upon him
> in humility and silent terror?

The segment airing that day recounted the sinking of a rickety, dangerously overloaded barge that capsized and broke apart in rough seas, drowning hundreds of passengers. Sharks encircled the vessel, attacking hapless passengers and gorging on their flesh. The sea was red with blood.

One passenger, a young woman, did not panic, though. Using a technique she'd learned in the Marines, she blew air into her pants legs, tied them, and used them to float. Adrift for days, she was finally sighted and rescued: disoriented, exhausted, and famished, on the cusp of death, yet still alive.

Can anyone doubt that this young woman prayed, or that her pleas were answered? I dare the obdurate unbeliever to ask *her* who God is.

No two people are alike, nor do they think alike. And no two persons' experience of God is the same. So too, each one's prayer life will be different, reflecting the diversity of individual character, belief, emotional state, and daily life. The form is never important. Personally, my wife and I have found that praying together in the morning is crucial to getting through our day, and it has become part of a natural rhythm in our married life.

In his *Letters and Papers from Prison*, Dietrich Bonhoeffer goes so far as to say that prayer (or the absence of it) can decide the outcome of our day. When we waste time, when we give in to temptations in thought or deed, when we feel weary or uninspired or lazy, the root of it often lies in our neglect of prayer. Seventeenth-century English cleric Thomas Fuller, who obviously felt much the same, wrote that for him "prayer is the key of the day and the lock of the night." And journalist Mike Aquilina, a friend, says prayer is an indispensable part of his day, too:

> My work, my joys, my sufferings, and my leisure, I offer to God, and I try to keep an awareness of his presence throughout the day. In this, I've found it especially helpful to make a regular commitment of time specifically for prayer. So I get up early, and as my first act of the morning I offer God my day. While the family is still asleep, I spend a half-hour in quiet conversation with God, speaking with him about the day's coming events. Then I usually meditate on a chapter from the New Testament and perhaps a few pages from some other spiritual book. The most important part of my daily prayer is my attendance at Mass. At some point in the afternoon, I usually spend another half-hour in quiet prayer. In the evening, we pray the rosary together, and I close my evening by examining the day's events in the presence of God, by offering him thanks and contrition.
>
> That's an outline of my daily discipline, but that's not my prayer, any more than a pile of my organs and bones

would be me. Prayer is something living. Prayer is seeing God in every person. Prayer is knowing I am wrong – and expressing my contrition – when I lash out in anger at my friends. Prayer is all of the communication, verbal and non-verbal, in my love relationship with the Lord. I think of it in comparison with my other great love, my wife: our communication encompasses our formal marriage vows, our casual conversation, our moments with the kids, our moments alone, winks across a crowded room, smiles across the table, sexual intimacy, and some set phrases or gestures of affection that we never tire of repeating. Sometimes, our communication is just knowing we are together, whether we're working in tandem, or sitting beside one another, each reading a different book. My communication with God encompasses a similar range of expressions – the set phrases, the quiet conversation, the gestures, but also my partaking in the sacrament of the Eucharist.

Like many others I have quoted, Clement of Alexandria says that prayer is a conversation with God. The more I think about this definition, the more I realize how good it is; namely, prayer does indeed include both talking and listening, ongoing dialogue and periods of silence, moments of happy fulfillment and hours of doubt and sorrow. The definition is also good because it helps to remind us that our communication need not be formal or "fixed"; on the contrary, it proceeds like a conversation: naturally, spontaneously, and freely. The longing for it will simply be there, just like the natural bodily needs we call hunger and thirst.

Psalm 42 opens: "As the deer longs for flowing streams, so longs my soul for you, O God." This is a wonderful image of how the thirsty soul turns to God – never satisfied by one drink, but continually turning back to him, over and over, to gain new strength.

John, a fellow pastor, says that for him and his wife, Gwen, prayer is not something they discuss or even need to remember—and certainly not something to be fitted into a busy schedule. To them it is simply second nature.

Ever since we were married, we have read something of a spiritual nature and prayed together—every morning and every night. We take turns saying the prayer. Turning inward like this has been a tremendous help to us personally, because it helps us to focus on the needs of others around us and throughout the world. The communal prayer of the church (including the silent, personal prayer of its members) has also meant a great deal to us, and we have seen remarkable things happen as a result of it, though often in a quiet way. Prayers of intercession are very important, but I believe the constant, if largely subconscious, attitude of thankfulness to God—for all his gifts, his protection, and his leading—is even more significant.

When I think about my life, I am deeply thankful to God for his guidance over the years, in spite of the many times I strayed. The sense that God is leading me step by step has always given me peace of heart. It was nothing I earned; it was pure grace.

Of course, there have also been periods in my life when I thought I knew where God was leading me, and then I found I was on the wrong track.

Now I am old and feel I have gained little in wisdom, if any. I still have my weaknesses. I am still John! The things I found important as a young man remain important to me today: economic and social justice, peace, and the brotherhood of man. Yet there are a few things that have become increasingly meaningful: prayer, faithfulness to my calling, and, most of all, thankfulness. How easily I become selfish and concerned with superficial things!

To me, prayer is by no means a matter of always going on one's knees. The essential elements are simply thanking God, praising him, waiting for him to lead, and trusting him. Trust gives me peace, for I know that if I leave everything in his hands, his will, whatever it is, will become reality in my life.

We have no idea how much prayer can accomplish. Tennyson once wrote, "More things are wrought by prayer than this world dreams of." Johann Christoph Blumhardt's life was threatened several times. One night a man slipped into Blumhardt's attic and hid, knife in hand, with the intention of murdering him in his sleep. While lying in wait, he heard Blumhardt pray and found his faith so disarming that he fled the house. The next morning Blumhardt found a letter from the man on his doorstep, confessing his intentions and telling him that this prayer had changed his life.

Prayer is each individual's contribution to his church and to the world. If we care about the spiritual life, we will live in active prayer. This should be a comfort for the sick, the elderly, and others who cannot do much else but pray. I have often thought that what they are doing for God and for the world is more important than what we who are healthy and active do all day. Dick and Lois Ann, neighbors for over forty years, say that as they age, they have begun to realize the same.

> Prayer has always been part of our marriage, but in the last years, as we have looked more often toward the end of our lives, it has gained in importance. We have been much moved by the writings of Thomas Merton, and through him, those of St. John of the Cross. Our prayers have

become more contemplative, a more natural part of our daily life and work, and we have had deeper experiences of inner quiet before God. We have learned to use silence to praise God.

It has been said that at the end of life one stands between time and eternity. In a sense, this is always true. But we have also found that through prayer, the boundaries between life and death, time and eternity, are taken away, and we can live in direct contact with God.

23.

faithfulness

At the dawn of creation, God and man were friends. In the cool of the evening, God walked with Adam and Eve. The earth was at peace. Even after the expulsion from the Garden of Eden, God and man were still close: Noah talked to God, listened to him, and obeyed him; so did Abraham and Moses. God accompanied the children of Israel as a pillar of fire by night and a pillar of cloud by day as they traveled the long years through the desert. Throughout the Bible, men and women talked with God—and God talked with them.

As the centuries rolled by, humankind drifted away from God, building towers of Babel to their own honor. But God remained faithful; he continued to speak and to listen, sometimes directly, sometimes through visions and angels. His voice can still be heard, if we are only attuned to hear it: in the voices that speak out above the hatred and greed, violence and dissention everywhere—voices that exhort us to rediscover life in relation to him.

Today religion appears to be everywhere, and millions of sincere people affirm a belief in God. Yet too many set other gods beside him: money and materialism, science and technology. It is not too much to say that as a culture, we have divorced ourselves entirely from him. It is true that there are those who seek God and experience his working in their lives in profound ways; yet all in all, it seems to me that today's society is a house of cards that could collapse with the next gust of wind.

The earth needs renewal, humanity needs renewal, and each of us needs renewal. But until the heavens open up, so to speak, it will not take place. There are hours of God for the whole world, when God shakes the nations. In our personal lives, too, there are hours when God comes close and speaks directly to us. I believe we are in an hour of God right now: he is shaking whole nations to the roots, and the forces of good and evil are pitted against each other in a tremendous spiritual battle. What is God telling us? Are we listening? God longs to save humankind from its suffering, but in the first place from the sin that causes it. All the more we need to be faithful to him and turn to him in prayer, asking him to intervene in history.

Because God loves us, he wants each one of us to live life to the full: he sent us Jesus to give us life, "that we might have it abundantly." Therefore, despite our willfulness and sinfulness, he reaches down to us again and again. And just as we have been given the privilege of free will, so we have the ability to reach up to him, as the following story from Dan, a close friend, illustrates.

The very word "prayer" conjures up for me a long journey marked by God's intervention, love, and faithfulness. I cannot think of prayer without thinking of friendship with God—a friendship I have broken time and again, but which, for reasons that remain a mystery to me, God began and has maintained.

I was raised in a church-going family, but went to services with something akin to bewilderment. The candles, the solemn music, the robes, the rituals, and the prayers to a person I couldn't see and didn't know—all were part of an experience I couldn't understand.

If I had attempted innocent prayers as a child, all of that was left behind by the time I was sixteen. I became totally preoccupied with the experiences unfolding for a teenager in the early seventies. My generation took the worst of the sixties and ran with it. By the end of my senior year in high school, I was heavily addicted to alcohol and marijuana.

My superficial existence was shattered when, at the age of seventeen, I was in a near-fatal car accident. Three other friends and myself had been out bar-hopping, and our Cadillac hit a tree at about forty miles an hour. I was in the passenger seat without a seatbelt and was flung, face first, into the dashboard. My recollections of that night are nothing but vague, brief glimpses. Of the four of us, I was hurt the worst, and should have been dead or at least unconscious.

It would be weeks before I could stand on my shaking legs and see my own blackened, unrecognizable face in the mirror. When I finally returned home, I was weak and dazed. Why had I survived all that? What did my teenage world mean now? I thought about the night of the accident, about my unexplained consciousness. In some dim sense, I think I realized for the first time that something—or someone—else had been with me.

Life went on, and by the time college rolled around, I was wallowing in that volatile mix of teenage pride and insecurity. On my first trip home from college (Thanksgiving vacation) I learned that my father was abandoning my mother for another woman. My mom told me about this through a veil of tears. My world went black. I was at the peak of confusion myself, but I had to watch, helpless, as my mother sank further and further into despair, numbing her agony with bottles of rum, weeping in the darkness on the basement steps. For days, my father lay curled up on the sofa in a fetal position, covering himself completely with a blanket, motionless, catatonic, as he warred with his own conscience. When he finally emerged, he told me, "You're not going to have your daddy around anymore." My mother pleaded with him to stay, at least for the sake of us children, but he only said, "They'll survive."

Over the next years I felt a growing certainty that somebody was watching me; that there was something other than my own dark world that also had a claim to reality. But I blocked any deeper reflection on it for a long time.

I remember vividly the first time I ever connected that "something other" with a person I could relate to. I had been out doing drugs and found myself sitting alone in a schoolyard in the middle of the night. The effects had worn off, it was dark, but the lights of the city twinkled below the hill where I was perched. I became aware that someone was with me, someone familiar, who knew my pain, my agony, my despair. I did not know then what this person demanded of me, or even why he was with me. I was only certain that he knew me and was watching over me.

Then, one day, my life changed forever. My mom had given me a book about the apostle Luke, who cared for people dying of the plague in the holds of ships. I found myself confronted with an unexplainable reality. Here was a man who, for no apparent reason, exposed himself to deadly illness to comfort the dying. There was no earthly reason to explain what Luke did. It was as if I'd hit a wall. I was alone in my apartment. I picked up the Bible my Mom had sent me and began to read. Suddenly, all the broken, filthy, shattered pieces of my life came together, as if I could see them all at once. And I knew that God could see them, too. Yes, he had been with me through all those years of darkness and pain and confusion. I hadn't been alone after all. I was overcome by the realization that there *is* a God in heaven, and that, more than anything else, God is Love. I did not see Jesus with my eyes in those moments, but he was in the room with me—a powerful, living presence. I did not hear words spoken, yet he spoke directly into my heart. It is impossible to describe the compassion I felt radiating from the living person of Christ. Tears streamed down my face—not for minutes, but for days, on and off.

Even as I write, tears come to my eyes as I realize how I've betrayed that compassion again and again. Jesus had come to me as a friend. God is a friend, someone I can talk to. And now his suffering made sense in a way that was both wondrous and mysterious. That battered, bloodied body I'd seen hanging from crosses in church as a young boy was something I could identify with. Though no other human being can grasp the inner and outer pain of the crucifixion, I felt as if we were brothers. He knew what I had gone through, and more—far, far more.

Those days of revelation years ago changed my entire perspective on life. Suddenly, I had hope; I saw the world, and the people in it, with new eyes. And I began to talk with God as a friend, to pray. I know that my life was changed because of the prayers of my mother and many others who hurt for me. Prayer is that way—it feeds on itself, lives are transformed, and prayers from renewed hearts reach outward to others, affecting more lives. Jesus said, "If you remain in me, whatever you ask in my name will be granted." I have seen this promise fulfilled many times, in ways I could never have imagined.

Over time, I was led away from my own depravity and toward the light that had broken into my life. I still go through plenty of struggles with the selfishness and impurity that bound me for so long. There are times when I am almost overwhelmed by the black thoughts and memories that crowd my mind relentlessly, costing me much sleep and peace of heart. Yet deep down, I trust in the fact that God knows my heart; he knows that I want only him. I take much courage from Jesus' words: "Blessed are the poor in spirit." Someday, I trust, I will be freed to the extent that I can also be included in his words, "Blessed are the pure in heart, for they shall see God."

Prayer is my lifeline. Whenever I focus wholeheartedly on the person of Christ and talk to him in the midst of inner battles, the power of evil is broken.

There have been times when I've wondered why God doesn't just give up on me. But of course, God isn't like that. He is faithful. My joy lies in the certainty that no matter what happens to us, or what we have to endure, we have been given a purpose far beyond ourselves. We can go forward knowing that our struggles and our prayers have meaning for others. And we can trust that their prayers have meaning for us.

I believe that, in the end, God will find the soul of every single person, as he found Dan. God is the "great Other" who is always reaching out to us. I have seen God's power at work in so many lives, and I refuse to believe that his power is restricted to the lives of just a few. Jesus said, "Ask what you will in my name, and it will be granted," and he meant it. It is up to us to take him at his word.

George MacDonald writes that it is as if all Christians held within them a wonderful secret, one that seems too good to be true, but must be true because it is so good. I would take MacDonald's thought one step further and say that not just the Christian, but every person on earth, has within him or her that wonderful secret—a seed of love that can grow and blossom for God.

James, an old friend now in his eighties, writes:

Over many years, I have come to feel that prayer is more of a relationship than an activity, less something I do, and more who I am. Though I am aware of my shortcomings, it is my longing and prayer to know God's will and to do it. More and more I realize my own powerlessness and sinfulness, and so I need to ask especially for his Spirit. My faith in God has to undergird every decision and every activity. Just as there are natural laws that govern our physical life, the law of love must govern our inner life. Prayer will then become a natural, underlying assumption in all I think and do.

A person who prays is like a servant who waits on God. Like a faithful servant, he must be capable of changing, always watching the hands of his master, never knowing what the next hour may bring. His prayer will be spontaneous – a natural expression of his love to his maker.

If our prayer life is living, it will be free, because the spirit of life is moving within our hearts. Then too, it will be genuine, not an empty rite.

We are told, "Come to me, all you who are burdened," and we may trustingly bring to God all our fears and worries, our desperation and anger. But if we approach him with agendas, with plans and ideas – if we press for the answer we want to hear – we will surely be disappointed. Only when we drop our own programs and come before God like children, whether crying for help or groaning in pain, laughing (or weeping) with joy, is he sure to hear us.

To truly understand the meaning and power of prayer is a journey that never ends. It is a thirsting for truth, a hungering for righteousness. In a lifetime of searching, we may only catch a glimpse of light, a hint of truth. This attitude of openness, of seeking, is the beginning. Reverence before the greatness of God, coupled with humility and sincerity, will lead us to childlike trust in him and faith in his answers. This is the greatest gift of life on earth: the possibility of a direct and constant relationship with God through prayer.

God is life, rich and overflowing life, and he is also love. His eternal will is to draw us all into his life, into his love.

God seeks constantly to lift us out of our petty selves into the domain of his love. That is why he stepped out of himself and opened his heart to us. Incredibly, we insignificant beings are the objects of his concern! Out of the incomprehensible love of his heart, he loves each one of us quite personally.

God wants us to know his heart, to accept his word, to affirm his will and carry it out. He also longs for us to respond personally to him, by worshiping him in the freeing spirit of consecration that grasps the essential and then puts it into living practice.

Eberhard Arnold

The Psalmist asks: where does my help come from? And he answers his own question: from God, the maker of heaven and earth. Therefore, he lifts his eyes to the mountains, "whence cometh help."

other titles by the author

Why Forgive?

No matter the weight of our bitterness, forgiving is the surest way to get out from under it. In this book survivors of crime, betrayal, abuse, bigotry, and war share their amazing stories to challenge and encourage others wherever they are on the road to healing.

Be Not Afraid

In this hope-filled book, ordinary men and women offer hard-won insights on dealing with uncertainty, loss, grief, and the fear of death. Through their real-life stories, Arnold shows how suffering can be given meaning, and despair overcome.

Why Children Matter

Raising a child has never been more challenging. Arnold offers time-tested wisdom and common-sense advice on what children need most, what holds a family together, and how to rediscover the joy of parenting.

Sex, God & Marriage

A refreshing new look at sex, love, and marriage that sees past the usual issues and gets to the root: our relationship with God, and the defining power of that bond over all other relationships.

Seeking Peace

Where can we find peace of heart and mind—with ourselves, with others, and with God? Arnold draws on the wisdom of some exceptional (and some very ordinary) people who have found peace in surprising places.

Their Name is Today

Arnold highlights drastic changes in the way our society treats children. But he also brings together the voices of dedicated parents and educators who are finding creative ways to give children the time and space they need to grow.

Rich in Years

Why shouldn't growing older be rewarding? Arnold wants us to rediscover the spiritual riches that age has to offer. Having personally faced the trials of aging, and having decades of pastoral experience, he knows what older people and caregivers can do to make the most of the journey.

Plough Publishing House, www.plough.com, 1-800-521-0800
151 Bowne Drive, PO Box 398, Walden, NY 12586, USA
Brightling Rd, Robertsbridge, East Sussex TN32 5DR, UK
4188 Gwydir Highway, Elsmore, NSW 2360, AU

acclaim for the author

The Houston Chronicle
Arnold is thought-provoking and soul-challenging…
He writes with an eye-opening simplicity that zings the heart.

Eugene Peterson, author
With so much junk spirituality on the market today,
it is positively refreshing to come upon Arnold's books…
They are solid and mature, devoid of ego, embracing
of community and ambiguity and integrity.

Madeleine L'Engle, author
We recognize ourselves in Arnold's poignant stories,
and our recognition helps us toward deeper understanding.

Peter Kreeft, author
Arnold is clear, compassionate, uncompromising…
he writes straight from (and to) the heart.

Publishers Weekly
Johann Christoph Arnold writes in a prayerful and simple way.

Lewis Smedes, author
Arnold's writing is simple, transparent, and caring.

Benedict Groeschel, CFR, Archdiocese of New York
With their customary blend of Gospel faith and personal
sharing, Arnold's books offer spiritual reading at its best.

Donna Schaper, author
Arnold's writing embraces despair, but it also restores
confidence.

Dick Staub, Host, The Dick Staub Show
Arnold's stories are touching and honest…and model vital
themes in a profound way.

Jonathan Kozol, author
Arnold's writing is unpretentious and transcendent.

Sam Hall, WQXR/New York
Arnold's writing is wonderful, touching, and reassuring.

Mairead Maguire, Nobel Peace Prize Laureate
Arnold inspires each of us to seek peace within our own
hearts…His writing gives hope that we can find wholeness,
happiness, and harmony, which is after all the fulfillment of
God's plan for humanity.

Richard John Neuhaus, First Things
Arnold's message is demanding and exhilarating, which is
what disciples of Jesus should expect.

Thomas Howard, author
The candor, simplicity, and humanity of Arnold's writing
should recommend it to an exceedingly wide reading public.

David Steindl-Rast, Mount Saviour Monastery
Arnold speaks out of a tradition of radical discipleship…
His writings are living water for gasping fish.

Alex J. Brunett, Archbishop Emeritus of Seattle
Arnold offers readers wonderful insights into the meaning of
true Christianity…his anecdotal materials are sure to find an
echo in the hearts of readers, no matter where they are on the
spectrum of faith.

Joan Brown Campbell, National Council of Churches
Arnold's approach is cogent, well-reasoned…some may
disagree with this or that conclusion, but all will acknowledge
his sincerity.

Bernard Häring, author
Arnold's writing is a convincing testimony to a truly
ecumenical spirit. Readers will be grateful for the depth
and insights of this outstanding author.